# ImageMagick Tricks

## Web Image Effects from the Command Line and PHP

Unleash the power of ImageMagick with this fast, friendly tutorial and tips guide

**Sohail Salehi**

PUBLISHING

BIRMINGHAM - MUMBAI

# ImageMagick Tricks
## Web Image Effects from the Command Line and PHP

First published: June 2006

Production Reference: 2150606

Published by Packt Publishing Ltd.
32 Lincoln Road
Olton
Birmingham, B27 6PA, UK.

ISBN 1-904811-86-8

www.packtpub.com

Cover Image by www.visionwt.com

# Credits

**Author**

Sohail Salehi

**Reviewers**

Sven Henckel

Gabe Schaffer

Anthony Thyssen

**Technical Editor**

Rushabh Sanghavi

**Editorial Manager**

Dipali Chittar

**Development Editor**

David Barnes

**Indexer**

Mithil Kulkarni

**Proofreader**

Chris Smith

**Production Coordinator**

Manjiri Nadkarni

**Cover Designer**

Manjiri Nadkarni

# About the Author

**Sohail Salehi** was born in Mashad, Iran, on March 18, 1975. He graduated in Software Engineering from Mashad University in 2000. In recent years, Sohail has contributed to over 20 books, mainly in programming and computer graphics. He has written frequent articles for "0 & 1 Magazine", an IT magazine from Ferdowsi University. You can find a complete list of his work at www.sohail2d.com. In the past he has worked as a Chairman in the IT department of various universities including Mashad, Ferdowsi, and the Industrial Management University. Currently he is working on the IT training standards for the Iranian "Work and Science Organisation" 2005-2006 period.

Many thanks to my lovely wife Ghazal for being so kind to me during writing this book.

Many, many thanks to every one at Packt who helped me create such a great book.

Thanks to my very dear friend David Barnes for starting things off from the beginning, helping me nail down the concept, and accompanying me during various parts of this book.

# About the Reviewers

**Sven Henckel** studied media informatics at the University for Practical Business Studies in Gütersloh, Germany. His diploma thesis was about the automatic generation of layout documents like QuarkXPress and Adobe InDesign. Before studying he worked as a developer and consultant for web applications. He currently works as an IT project manager for a European media service provider. He has developed a quality assurance system in which ImageMagick plays a very important role. Through the years he has attained specialized knowledge in the fields of Java, PHP, SQL, XML, and PDF. Moreover, he is interested in Open Source software, communication, and design.

**Gabe Schaffer** has a degree in computer science from Case Western Reserve University in Cleveland, Ohio where he resides. He has been programming for over 20 years, has been doing photography for 10 years, and does both as a freelancer. He uses ImageMagick for automating digital photo labs.

I would like to thank Maggie for putting up with my late nights reviewing this book.

**Anthony Thyssen** is a UNIX and Linux Systems Expert with an interest in image processing tools for UNIX since 1996, and has released an unoffical patched version of the old NetPBM graphic tool suite. He has been a user of the command-line version of ImageMagick since its inception. In recent years he developed a Image Magick version 6 Examples website, `http://www.cit.gu.edu.au/~anthony/graphics/imagick6/`, as a practical users' manual for both new and old users of ImageMagick. He has also been involved in the debugging and development of the IM core software, specifically in the areas of Alpha Compositing and GIF animation optimization.

# Table of Contents

# Preface

ImageMagick ™ was introduced in 1999 by ImageMagick Studio LLC for the first time. It is a graphical application used for performing image processing tasks. It is a powerful collection of tools and libraries to read, write, and manipulate images in about 100 formats.

In this book, I'll show how to use the various ImageMagick utilities to create amazing artwork from the command line. You may find doing some image processing tasks with this program is more convenient than using other solutions, like Adobe Photoshop.

Let me give you an example. How do you resize about 3000 photos of different sizes and formats and place a watermark on them? This question led me to examine ImageMagick for the first time and after a while I found it to be a powerful and easy-to-learn application.

You may not believe how easily ImageMagick can do it for you. With a single command you can resize, watermark, add effects, frame, arrange, convert, format, and do many more tasks on a single image or a bunch of various images.

To cut a long story short, I think it is the best command-line image processing application that I've ever seen. It is more than a command-line application. If you are a programmer using compilers like C, Delphi, Python, Perl, and so on or even server-side languages like PHP, then you can find your favourite ImageMagick API for your compiler.

Due to space limitaion, this book concentrates just on command-line utilities. Maybe in the future we will publish titles on other ImageMagick APIs.

# What This Book Covers

*Chapter 1* is an introduction, which provides you with a brief history about Imagemagick and its capabilities.

*Chapter 2* contains useful steps for installing and configuring ImageMagick. There are some good resources for downloading the application—based on your OS—too.

*Chapter 3* covers the `convert` and `mogrify` utilities. You can find practical workshops in this chapter.

*Chapter 4* covers the `composite` and `montage` utilities and their role in combining and presenting images.

*Chapter 5* mainly focuses on input (`import` utility) and output (`display` utility) in ImageMagick. There are some descriptions about obtaining useful information from images using `identify`.

*Chapter 6* teaches you how to create animations using ImageMagick.

*Chapter 7* contains brief information about the ImageMagick command line programming language—`conjure`. Moreover in this chapter the `compare` utility, which compares the differences between two images of the same size, visually and mathematically will be studied too.

*Chapters 8, 9, and 10* cover some practical web projects including building a confirmation-code box, online customized e-cards, and online customized templates (for a book cover).

*Appendix A* will show you how to install and use new fonts. There are some free resources for fonts and images too.

*Appendix B* covers the compression and quality trade-off in ImageMagick.

# Conventions

In this book, you will find a number of styles of text that distinguish between different kinds of information. Here are some examples of these styles, and an explanation of their meaning.

There are three styles for code. Code words in text are shown as follows: "We can include other contexts through the use of the `include` directive."

A block of code will be set as follows:

```
[default]
exten => s,1,Dial(Zap/1|30)
exten => s,2,Voicemail(u100)
exten => s,102,Voicemail(b100)
exten => i,1,Voicemail(s0)
```

When we wish to draw your attention to a particular part of a code block, the relevant lines or items will be made bold:

```
[default]
exten => s,1,Dial(Zap/1|30)
exten => s,2,Voicemail(u100)
exten => s,102,Voicemail(b100)
exten => i,1,Voicemail(s0)
```

Any command-line input and output is written as follows:

```
convert rectangles.jpg -resize 900% rect_resized.jpg
```

**New terms** and **important words** are introduced in a bold-type font. Words that you see on the screen, in menus or dialog boxes for example, appear in our text like this: "clicking the **Next** button moves you to the next screen".

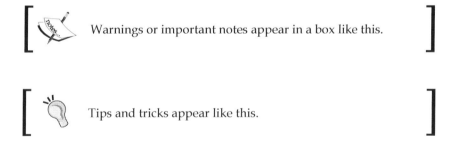

Warnings or important notes appear in a box like this.

Tips and tricks appear like this.

# Reader Feedback

Feedback from our readers is always welcome. Let us know what you think about this book, what you liked or may have disliked. Reader feedback is important for us to develop titles that you really get the most out of.

To send us general feedback, simply drop an email to feedback@packtpub.com, making sure to mention the book title in the subject of your message.

If there is a book that you need and would like to see us publish, please send us a note in the **SUGGEST A TITLE** form on www.packtpub.com or email suggest@packtpub.com.

If there is a topic that you have expertise in and you are interested in either writing or contributing to a book, see our author guide on www.packtpub.com/authors.

## Customer Support

Now that you are the proud owner of a Packt book, we have a number of things to help you to get the most from your purchase.

## Downloading the Example Code for the Book

Visit http://www.packtpub.com/support, and select this book from the list of titles to download any example code or extra resources for this book. The files available for download will then be displayed.

## Errata

Although we have taken every care to ensure the accuracy of our contents, mistakes do happen. If you find a mistake in one of our books—maybe a mistake in text or code—we would be grateful if you would report this to us. By doing this you can save other readers from frustration, and help to improve subsequent versions of this book. If you find any errata, report them by visiting http://www.packtpub.com/support, selecting your book, clicking on the **Submit Errata** link, and entering the details of your errata. Once your errata have been verified, your submission will be accepted and the errata added to the list of existing errata. The existing errata can be viewed by selecting your title from http://www.packtpub.com/support.

## Questions

You can contact us at questions@packtpub.com if you are having a problem with some aspect of the book, and we will do our best to address it.

# 1
# Introduction

In 1999 the ImageMagick Studio LLC developed a graphical application named ImageMagick for working on images. ImageMagick is a powerful collection of tools and libraries to read, write, and manipulate images in close to a hundred formats.

The question, is what is the point of using ImageMagick when there are so many professional image processing programs like Adobe Photoshop or Macromedia Freehand? Maybe one good reason is ImageMagick's powerful utilities and interfaces.

From a user's point of view, we may need a program to do a set of specific tasks (like resizing, labeling, framing, format converting, and much more) on the images that are located in a given URL with a single command. You may not believe how easily ImageMagick can do this for you.

Using ImageMagick we can create and edit images dynamically and show the result online on our desired URLs or locally on our computer. Besides popular transformations like resize, crop, rotate, flip, and so on, we can also execute image editing processes like inserting text, sharpen, blur, and color correction, and much more with ImageMagick's internal utilities by using simple command-line scripts.

Moreover, there are some excellent tools and programs that can be used for adding special effects to images. These effects include popular ones like border, blur, composite, implode, explode, and some artistic effects like detect edges, add noise, adaptive threshold, charcoal, oil paint, negate, shade, and plasma.

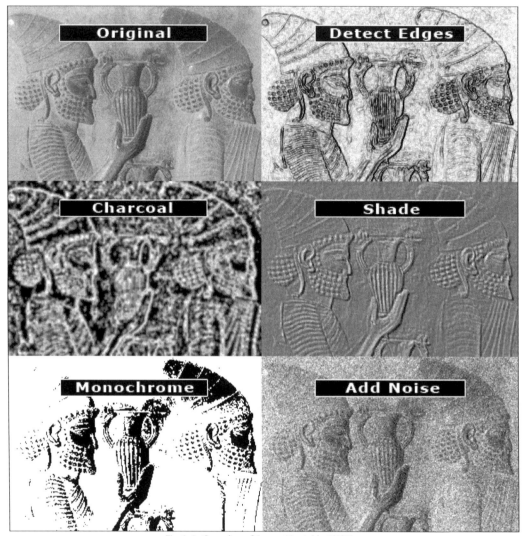

Fig 1-1: Samples of ImageMagick's Abilities

Another interesting feature of ImageMagick is its ability to work on animated file formats. It is possible to use all the ImageMagick effects available for still images on animated formats. In addition, there are some facilities that can be used for converting a group of still images to an animated sequence.

Making an animated graphic file is possible with a single ImageMagick command. Moreover, it is possible to show all single frames of a directory in a sequenced, animated order.

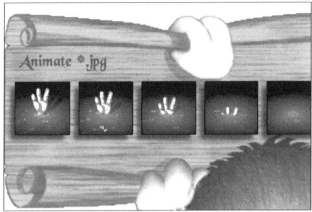

Fig 1-2: With the Animate *.jpg Command we can Animate a Directory of JPEG Images

Screen capturing is another useful ImageMagick feature. With this ability you can capture the current active window, the entire screen, or any rectangular portion of the screen and save it as an image.

Fig 1-3: Using the Import Utility we can: a) Capture the Entire Screen b) Capture just the Active Window
c) Capture a Selected Portion of the Current Screen

Due to various ImageMagick interfaces and tools, we can perform various image processing operations from the command line, or from our favorite programming language like C, C++, Perl, Java, PHP, Python, or Ruby. Moreover, a high-quality 2D renderer is included, which provides a subset of SVG capabilities.

# ImageMagick Features

There are so many capabilities you can work with in ImageMagick! We are going to study the most popular of them during the following chapters and then we will see how to use these features as programmers in our practical projects. Some of the topics and features that will be studied in this book are summarized as follows:

- **Format Conversion**: Convert an image from one format to another (about 100 formats supported)

- **Text & Comments**: Inserting descriptive or artistic text in images

- **Transformations**: Resize, rotate, crop, flip, and flop images

- **Color Correction:** Define threshold, reduce color, and color conversion for images

- **Background**: Create beautiful backgrounds and canvases

- **Thumbnail and Frame**: Create a framed thumbnail of an image

- **Transparency**: Create a transparent image for use on the World Wide Web

- **Animation**: Create a GIF animation sequence from a group of images

- **Composite**: Combine several images to create a composite image

- **Montage**: Generate a thumbnail index of a list of images

- **Special Effects**: Add artistic filters like charcoal, monochrome, and so on to an image

- **Multifunctioning**: Execute a group of tasks with a single script on entire directories of images

- **Image Identification**: Describe the format of the image and attributes

- **File Management**: Retrieve, list, or print files from a remote network site

# ImageMagick's Core Utilities

The real power of ImageMagick comes from its utilities. In fact with the help of these utilities we are able to do any reading, writing, and manipulating tasks on images. There are always third-party utilities that add more power to ImageMagick but the core utilities of this package are discussed below.

## Display

We can expect any image viewing and managing functionality including load, print, write to file, zoom, copy a region of the image, paste a region to the image, crop, show histogram, and so on from this utility.

## Convert

The main task of the `Convert` utility as its name suggests is converting image formats. We can use `Convert` for more functions, like making thumbnails of images, simulating a charcoal drawing, colorizing the image with the fill color, embossing an image, specifying a clipping mask, morphing an image sequence, and simulating an oil painting too.

# Import

The `Import` utility is used to capture the screen and convert it to a file. We can specify a single window, the entire screen, or any rectangular portion of the screen for capturing.

For saving as a file we have options to set the preferred number of colors in the image, the type of colorspace, annotate an image with a comment, add coder/decoder-specific options, and assign a label to an image.

# Animate

For showing animated formats or a sequence of still images we use the `Animate` utility. One of the important features of `Animate` is its capability for color reduction to match the color resolution of the workstation. We can show any full color images on a weak display unit (like a monochrome one).

# Composite

The `Composite` utility has a number of unique techniques for combining several separate images and making a composite result. Images can be composited together with the following schemes: Over, In, Out, Atop, Xor, Plus, Minus, Difference, Multiply, and Bumpmap. We will study them in detail in Chapter 4.

# Montage

This arranges a group of images into a single image or page and can apply ambiences such as border and shadow to them. This is useful for creating thumbnail images or a gallery effect. We will see how to use this feature in Chapter 4.

# Mogrify

`Mogrify` is mainly used for image transformation. These transformations include image scaling, image rotation, color reduction, and others. The main difference between `Mogrify` and other utilities is that it overwrites the result on the original image.

# Conjure

Do you have an aversion to popular ImageMagick programming languages like Perl, C, C++, PHP, and so on? If yes then you can use the Magick Scripting Language (MSL). This is an XML-based language and using the Conjure utility you can do any image processing activity without a Perl interpreter. First you write code for desired action and then call Conjure to execute that code. The code has a syntax similar to this:

```
<group>                             -- start a group of processing
    <image>                         -- create an image tag
    ...                             -- do something
    </image>                        -- end of process
    <image>                         -- create another image tag
    ...                             -- additional image manipulations
    </image>                        -- end of process
    <write filename="image.png" />  -- output
</group>                            -- dispose of both images
conjure -dimensions 400x400 mycode.msl
```

Between the <image> tags, we can insert reading, writing, and editing commands.

# Identify

For detecting more information about an image format we use the Identify utility. Besides other useful information like file name, file size, file format, width and height of the image, whether the image is color mapped and the number of colors in the image, and so on, it can detect if an image is corrupted.

# Interfaces

ImageMagick APIs (Application Programming Interface) are programming tools and libraries that programmers are definitely interested in. With the help of these tools, everyone can write his/her own image processing application for performing customized actions (See Fig 1-4). Some of these interfaces will be discussed with practical examples in the last few chapters of this book. PerlMagick, MagickWand, Magick++, and MagickWand for PHP are the interfaces covered in this book.

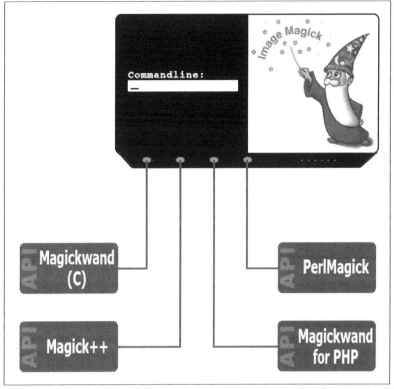

Fig 1-4: ImageMagick can Talk to every Programming Language using Various Programming Interfaces

# ImageMagick and X11 standard

ImageMagick is an X11 package. In computing, the X Window System (commonly known as X11) is a windowing system for image display. It is the standard graphical interface on OpenVMS, Unix, and Linux systems although Microsoft supports this standard as well.

This means that we can use ImageMagick in any platform that supports X11. So using ImageMagick, we can display any image on any workstation screen running an X server.

From a programmer's point of view, ImageMagick is a very flexible and portable package. As it has been written in the portable C programming language it will compile with any modern C compiler and no proprietary toolkits are required. Hence, every system can support it.

# Summary

In this chapter we learned that ImageMagick is an X11 image-processing package that can be widely used on many platforms.

The power of this application comes from its internal utilities. The most important ones are Display, Convert, Import, Conjure, Montage, Composite, Identify, Mogrify, and Animate.

There are some programming interfaces with ImageMagick that programmers can use for creating customized applications.

The programming interfaces that we are going to study in this book are PerlMagick, MagickWand, Magick++, and MagickWand for PHP.

In the next chapter we will study installing and configuring ImageMagick.

# Installation and Configuration

2

Like most other open-source applications, ImageMagick can be installed and configured on many platforms. In this chapter, we will discuss various installation processes and by the end of this chapter we will learn about:

- Getting ImageMagick
- ImageMagick installation requirements
- Installing ImageMagick from a source
- Installing ImageMagick from a binary
- Installing ImageMagick on supported platforms like:
    - **UNIX** platforms: **Linux, VMS, Mac OS, Solaris, FreeBSD**
    - **Windows**
- Fine tuning and required configuration after installation
- Handling bugs and errors

## Where to get ImageMagick

You can find many ImageMagick `ftp` and `http` download links on the Internet. But I suggest you download it from the original website, because the links in that site always lead you to the newest version of the program. Sometimes third-party websites update their links with a delay (unless they use the syndication solution for their download links).

Moreover, during the lifetime of a released version there are often some bugs and enhancements that are issued by ImageMagick users and based on these reports, the development team of ImageMagick will make any required changes and update the related link. Sometimes, in these cases other third-party websites may lose the chance to detect the updated features and resolved bugs in the current version.

You can get the newest suitable installer from `http://www.imagemagick.org/download`.

# What are the Installation Requirements?

Any successful image processing activity in ImageMagick needs enough swap memory and RAM. The amount of required memory depends on three factors:

- What is the action you are supposed to do?
- How many images you are working on?
- What is the size of the image you are working on?

As mentioned in the previous chapter, there are many actions that can be performed with ImageMagick. Some of them like resizing images need less system resources as compared to ones like working with PDF formats.

The number of images is another important factor. Working on a directory with hundreds of images is obviously different from handling a single file and needs much more memory.

The third factor is the size of the image you are working with. Bigger images need larger amount of memory. I installed and tested ImageMagick on several machines with various free resources and based on my experiments allocating 100 MB of disk space for swap memory on a computer with 128 MB of RAM will run the program without errors. Any more resources will enhance the program execution.

# Installation

After getting to the program download page we will see many download links. The question is what are these links for? And which one is suitable for me?

In fact, depending on the platform, there is a specific installer. At the time of writing this book, the installers are as follows.

## Binary Installers

**Platform**: Fedora Core 3 i386 RPM

**Download Links:**

`http://www.imagemagick.org/download/linux/fedora/i386/ImageMagick-6.2.6-5.i386.rpm`

`ftp://ftp.imagemagick.org/pub/ImageMagick/linux/fedora/i386/ImageMagick-6.2.6-5.i386.rpm`

**Platform**: Fedora Core 3 x86_64 RPM

**Download Links**:

```
http://www.imagemagick.org/download/linux/fedora/x86_64/ImageMagick-
6.2.5-5.x86_64.rpm
```

```
ftp://ftp.imagemagick.org/pub/ImageMagick/linux/fedora/x86_64/
ImageMagick-6.2.6-5.x86_64.rpm
```

**Platform**: Mac OS X

**Download Links**:

```
http://www.imagemagick.org/download/binaries/ImageMagick-powerpc-apple-
darwin8.5.0.tar.gz
```

```
ftp://ftp.imagemagick.org/pub/ImageMagick/binaries/ImageMagick-powerpc-
apple-darwin8.5.0.tar.gz
```

**Platform**: Solaris Sparc 2.10

**Download Links**:

```
http://www.imagemagick.org/download/binaries/ImageMagick-sparc-sun-
solaris2.10.tar.gz
```

```
ftp://ftp.imagemagick.org/pub/ImageMagick/binaries/ImageMagick-sparc-sun-
solaris2.10.tar.gz
```

**Platform**: FreeBSD 4.8

**Download links**:

```
http://www.imagemagick.org/download/binaries/ImageMagick-i386-unknown-
freebsd4.8.tar.gz
```

```
ftp://ftp.imagemagick.org/pub/ImageMagick/binaries/ImageMagick-i386-
unknown-freebsd4.8.tar.gz
```

**Platform**: Cygwin

**Download links**:

```
http://www.imagemagick.org/download/binaries/ImageMagick-i686-pc-cygwin.tar.gz
```

```
ftp://ftp.imagemagick.org/pub/ImageMagick/binaries/ImageMagick-i686-pc-
cygwin.tar.gz
```

**Platform**: Windows (Dynamic at 16 bits-per-pixel)

**Download links**:

```
http://www.imagemagick.org/download/binaries/ImageMagick-6.2.6-5-Q16-
windows-dll.exe
```

```
ftp://ftp.imagemagick.org/pub/ImageMagick/binaries/ImageMagick-6.2.6-5-
Q16-windows-dll.exe
```

**Platform**: Windows (Static at 16 bits-per-pixel)

**Download links**:

`http://www.imagemagick.org/download/binaries/ImageMagick-6.2.6-5-Q16-windows-static.exe`

`ftp://ftp.imagemagick.org/pub/ImageMagick/binaries/ImageMagick-6.2.6-5-Q16-windows-static.exe`

**Platform**: Windows (Dynamic at 8 bits-per-pixel)

**Download links**:

`http://www.imagemagick.org/download/binaries/ImageMagick-6.2.6-5-Q8-windows-dll.exe`

`ftp://ftp.imagemagick.org/pub/ImageMagick/binaries/ImageMagick-6.2.6-5-Q8-windows-dll.exe`

**Platform**: Windows (Static at 8 bits-per-pixel)

**Download links**:

`http://www.imagemagick.org/download/binaries/ImageMagick-6.2.6-5-Q8-windows-static.exe`

`ftp://ftp.imagemagick.org/pub/ImageMagick/binaries/ImageMagick-6.2.6-5-Q8-windows-static.exe`

# Source files

**Platforms**: All UNIX-like systems (Linux, FreeBSD, MacOS X, Solaris)

**Download link**:

`ftp://ftp.imagemagick.org/pub/ImageMagick/ImageMagick.tar.gz`

**Platform**: Windows

**Download link**:

`ftp://ftp.imagemagick.org/pub/ImageMagick/windows/ImageMagick-windows.zip`

As you can see the ImageMagick installation programs are categorized into two groups:

- Programs that install it from binaries
- Programs that install it from source

If you prefer to install the program with a few clicks and without any complicated settings, use one of the binary installers based on your platform. These installers are ready-to-run executable files that install ImageMagick with default settings. The required steps for installing them are provided in the next topic. After that you can omit the rest of this chapter and proceed to the next one.

Professionals who care about the specific settings and configuration usually make their ImageMagick application from the source. This process is a little tricky and we need a compiler for building the executable program.

# How to Install ImageMagick from Binaries

These installers are provided in either `.rpm`, `.tar.gz`, or `.exe`. For setting up the program just run the executable files or uncompress the `.tar.gz` ones. In general, these installers set up the default features but in some cases after installation we need to define the working path of the program for the system.

# How to Install from UNIX-like Binary Releases

An RPM file is a self-installing program that can be run from the command line. For example in order to install the `ImageMagick-6.2.3-5.i386.rpm` file on a Fedora platform just type the following command:

```
rpm -Uvh ImageMagick-6.2.3-5.i386.rpm
```

Installing a `.tar.gz` file is a little tricky. We have to determine the target path first. Then using a suitable utility, we have to uncompress the file in that directory. In the following example the Gzip utility is used for unpacking ImageMagick:

```
gzip -dc ImageMagick.tar.gz | tar -xf -
```

Alternatively, we can use:

```
tar -xvzf  ImageMagick.tar.gz
```

The final step includes defining certain environmental and system variable settings. First ensure that the ImageMagick `bin` subdirectory exists in the system executable path. Check the `PATH` environment variable and add the following line to it if it does not exist:

```
export PATH; PATH="$HOME/ImageMagick/bin:$PATH"
```

Moreover, the MAGICK_HOME environment variable should be set to the path where you previously extracted the ImageMagick files. For example:

```
export MAGICK_HOME="$HOME/ImageMagick-6.2.3"
```

You need to define another setting if your platform is Linux or Solaris. In these machines ImageMagick library files are unavailable unless you set the LD_LIBRARY_PATH environment variable as follows:

```
export LD_LIBRARY_PATH="$HOME/ImageMagick-6.2.3/lib"
```

## How to Verify the Program Installation

As you'll learn in Chapter 3 the Display utility is a program that is used for basic image processing activities. We use it here to check whether ImageMagick is working properly:

```
display logo.gif
```

If you see the ImageMagick logo after running this command, you can be sure of the program installation validity.

I prefer to use the following command to do this:

```
convert -version
```

It will show other useful information besides testing the correctness of the installation. Here is the output of this command:

**Version: ImageMagick 6.2.3 07/30/05 Q16 http://www.imagemagick.org
Copyright: Copyright (C) 1999-2005 ImageMagick Studio LLC**

## How to Install from a Windows Binary Release

Installing ImageMagick on Windows with a binary installer is as straightforward as any other Windows standard program installer. We will study the installation process step by step.

Although ImageMagick can be run on older versions of Windows, it's recommended that we use newer versions as some ImageMagick features work better with them.

For setting up the program, get the suitable binary file and double-click on it. A set of introductory dialogs will be shown consisting of a welcome message (Fig 2-1 a), a license agreement (Fig 2-1 b), information about the program (Fig 2-1 c), setting the destination for program installation (Fig 2-1 d) and finally choosing a name for the program folder on the Windows start menu (Fig 2-1 e).

Just click **Next** to go ahead and do not change anything unless you want to install ImageMagick on a specific path or decide to choose a different name for its start menu folder.

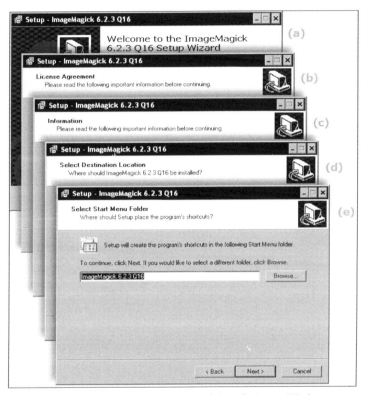

Fig 2-1: Primary Steps of ImageMagick Installation on Windows

The step shown in the next screenshot is very important.

In this dialog besides settings for making a shortcut icon on desktop, for associating image files with the ImageMagick Display utility and doing any necessary changes in path variable (in the `autoexec.bat` file), we can choose extra libraries, DLLs, and source files to be installed, so that ImageMagick can communicate with other programming languages such as C, C++, Perl, PHP, and so on via these interface files.

We will use these files in the future as an interface to the **ImageMagick** core features in our personal programs.

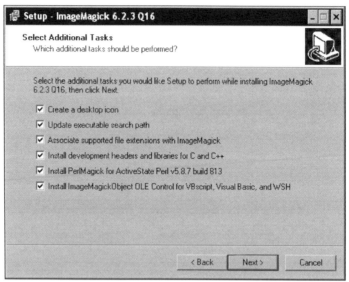

Fig 2-2: Choose to Install any Extra Programming Sources, DLLs, and Libraries

Look at the third option in this dialog. If you turn on this option file formats (like PostScript and MPEG) and extra image processing capabilities (like RAWTORLE and SANE for scanning images), which by default do not exist in ImageMagick, will be added to the program.

These features are called delegates and will be discussed in detail in Appendix A.

Click on the **Next** button after setting the options of this dialog and you will be led to the next dialog, which contains some informative contents including the path of the program destination plus current features that you have selected for installation.

Click on **Next** again and the installation process begins.

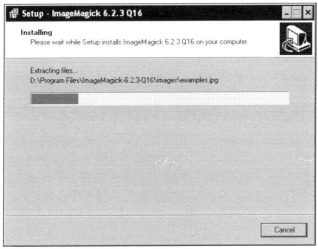
Fig 2-3: Installation Progress

At the end of installation, type **IMDISPLAY** in an MS-DOS command-prompt window and if you see the Display window utility, you are ready to read, write, and edit your images with ImageMagick.

# How to Install ImageMagick from Source

This type of installation needs some tools like external compilers and enough knowledge about compiler parameter settings and platform configuration. So it is strongly suggested that if you have enough programming knowledge and want to have in-depth control over ImageMagick features then you should install it from the source; otherwise install it from a binary source with a few commands or clicks (as described in the previous topic) and go to the next chapter. In general the process of installing ImageMagick from the source can be divided into three main steps:

- Uncompress the source files
- Make the program with a compiler
- Set the environmental configuration according to the platform

After installation there are some necessary system configurations without which the program may work incorrectly.

Keep in mind that installing ImageMagick from the source files means setting up the core features and utilities of the program version that you are going to make. For adding any extra delegates you need to get the related source files from third-party websites and compile them.

Before installing from source, always review recent changes to the ImageMagick distribution to find out what features have been built internally and what capabilities you need to add by yourself (or manage without!). Here is the link to the latest version of the program: http://www.imagemagick.org/script/changelog.php.

# Installing from a UNIX-like Source

The good news is the file that provides a UNIX-like source installer can be used for LINUX, Mac OS X, VMS, Solaris, and FreeBSD. So the uncompressing and making phases for all of these platforms are the same and we just need to know configuring issues for every platform.

Download the latest version from ftp://ftp.imagemagick.org/pub/ ImageMagick/ImageMagick.tar.gz and uncompress it using your unzip program:

```
gunzip -c ImageMagick.tar.gz | tar xvf -
```

or

```
tar -xvzf ImageMagick.tar.gz
```

From now on, you have a set of ImageMagick source files and folders, which should be compiled with specific options according to your platform.

## What are Makefiles?

In order to build ImageMagick, we need a tool to create the required Makefiles. Makefiles are predefined files that contain instructions and settings for building ImageMagick. We can create them with GNU Configure or X11 Imake.

## How to Use GNU Configure for Creating Makefiles

For users who prefer to define each preference and setting by themselves, GNU Configure is a good choice. This method is usually used for situations in which make configuration files are not available.

Simply type the following command and study the output:

```
./configure
```

Then if you prefer to change some settings like files to compile, compilation flags, or libraries, use the command line. Obviously you have to be familiar with compiler settings or you'll end up building processes with errors. (Studying compiler features and options is beyond the scope of this book.)

For example in the following command:

```
CC=-Xa CFLAGS=-g LIBS=-lposix ./configure
```

CC, CFLAGS, and LIBS define the name of the C compiler, compiler flags, and extra libraries required to link for program building respectively.

Moreover there are some options for the configure command that define the ImageMagick features and capabilities during compilation. We use –disable / --enable and –with / --without switches to tell the compiler which *features* and *packages* should be compiled for building the programs and which ones shouldn't.

Keep the following scheme in mind for disabling an option:

--disable-something is the same as --enable-something=no

--without-something is the same as --with-something=no

When you use --enable-something in order to enable a *feature*, the configure command enables the related ImageMagick code that already exists. When you use --with-something in order to enable a *package*, the configure script will search for its headers and build libraries. If these files are found by the compiler they will be included in the build process and ImageMagick will armed with the package.

By default, all features are disabled and all packages are enabled in a configure script. So if you prefer to change something in this code you will have to do it manually.

Type configure --help at the command line to see all available options for configure. Questions? Try the ImageMagick forums at http://studio.imagemagick.org/discussion-server/.

Here is a list of some popular options:

| Option | Description |
| --- | --- |
| --enable-16bit-pixel | enables 16 bit pixels (default is no) |
| --enable-lzw | enables LZW support (default is no) |
| --enable-prof | enables prof source profiling support (default is no) |
| --enable-shared | builds shared libraries (default is no) |
| --enable-static | builds static libraries (default is yes) |
| --enable-socks | enables use of SOCKS v5 library and 'rftp' |
| --enable-socks | enables SOCKS v5 proxy support (default is no) |
| --with-bzlib | enables BZLIB (default is yes) |

| Option | Description |
|---|---|
| --with-dps | enables Display Postscript (default is yes) |
| --with-fpx | enables FlashPIX (default is yes) |
| --with-frozenpaths | enables frozen delegate paths (default is yes) |
| --with-hdf | enables HDF (default is yes) |
| --with-jpeg | enables JPEG (default is yes) |

## Configure Command in Action

With a file named `magick.tmpl` you can further tweak some settings and configuration specially related to initializing environment variables for your platform. For example due to these settings, ImageMagick uses an eight bit color space (for various settings such as each red, green, blue, and transparent component). Therefore in the case of sixteen bit images their color data will be reduced to eight bits. If you prefer to work with sixteen bit colors you can make some changes in the `QuantumLeap` definition found in the `Magick.tmpl` body.

Another alternative is to use the `-enable-16bit` parameter in the `Configure` command and then build the program again as shown below:

```
make clean
make
```

The payback of this change is a memory usage increment (close to thirty percent) and slowing down the processing speed in some effects like Oil Painting, Segment, and so on.

# How to Use the Make Command for LINUX

The `Make` command definitely facilitates the installation process. Assuming that configuration files are available you can use this command. Using the `Make` command requires installing PerlMagick in a separate step.

With the `Make` command, we have no access to configuration options and installation progress will be approved with default settings. So it is strongly recommended to study the `magick/magick.h` and `magick/delegates.h` contents and declarations before installation to ensure that they are compatible with your system requirements.

The final important tip is to use an **ANSI**-compatible compiler for building ImageMagick or you will encounter fatal errors.

After taking these steps type the following command for compiling the program:

```
cd magick
make -k
cd..
make -k
```

At the end use the following command to verify installation:

```
display logo.gif
```

# How to Build ImageMagick for the VMS Platform

The basic steps to compile the program on VMS are same as the ones discussed previously. Once again check the `magick.h` contents for requirement issues and then enter the following commands:

```
@make
set display/create/node=node_name
```

In the `node_name` value place the DECnet X server that you are going to build the program on. Check the compilation validity with Display:

```
display logo.gif
```

Although there are standard packages included in ImageMagick for VMS, as before for building extra features like reading VMS JPEG, MPEG, TIFF, and XPM formats you have to download the related source files from `ftp://ftp.wizards.dupont.com/pub/ImageMagick/vms` (or other links that you know) and compile them separately.

# How to Build ImageMagick for the Macintosh Platform

There are some exceptions in the ImageMagick for Macintosh distribution. At the time of writing this book for the current version of the program (ImageMagick-6.2.3), the Display, Animate, and Import utilities are not supported.

After building the program on Mac OS X (Darwin) you have to set the `DYLD_LIBRARY_PATH` environment variable as follows or the program won't work properly:

```
export DYLD_LIBRARY_PATH="$HOME/ImageMagick-6.2.3/
lib"
```

## How to Build ImageMagick for the Windows Platform

After unpacking the source file on your computer there are two ways to compile it on Microsoft Visual Studio or on Borland C++.

Open the program project file (named `ImageMagick.dsw`) from the `VisualMagick/configure` folder and then build it in your compiler IDE (that is choose **Build | Build Solution in MS-Visual Studio IDE** and press **Next** on the following dialogs until the end.

Now set the environmental variables in `autoexec.bat`. Open `autoexec.bat` and add the following line to it:

```
SET DISPLAY=:0.0
```

Then make sure the ImageMagick extra executable files (like `gswin32` – `Ghostscript` for handling Postscript files) are in your `autoexec.bat` execution paths.

Finally, test the program functionality using Convert or other ImageMagick utilities.

# How to Handle Bugs and Errors

As of now, I can suggest two alternatives for handling bugs and errors during ImageMagick installation and configuration:

- You can join the ImageMagick support forum at: `http://studio.imagemagick.org/discussion-server/`.
- You can try to solve the problem with the `Configure` script.

## Dealing with Configuration Failures

The `Configure` script is useful for detecting program faults and errors during the installation process. So if you pay more attention to this command you may avoid later ImageMagick problems and malfunctions.

The `Configure` command has some mechanisms that check the existence and functionality of provided headers and libraries. The basic parameters that are used by `Configure` to test the source files (including header files `.h` and libraries `.lib`) are:

- The Compiler (CC)
- Compilation Flags (CFLAGS)
- Pre-processor Flags (CPPFLAGS)
- Linker Flags (LDFLAGS)

With the help of these parameters if any trouble is detected `Configure` will log it in the `config.log` file. So by viewing this file we can determine the cause of many program faults and resolve them.

Usually configuration failures have similar patterns and you can detect them immediately by spending a little time on them. For example a linker error (LDFLAGS -L/-R option) means that the `Configure` command cannot find the related plug-in `.lib` file. This means either the file does not exist or it is not in the linker search/run path. When a plug-in header file error is detected (CPPFLAGS -I option) it means that the `Configure` command cannot see it in the header file include path.

> With the *ldd* command in Solaris and Linux systems you can find out the libraries that ImageMagick depends on as follows:
>
> `ldd `which convert``

If you succeed in detecting and correcting the problem, remove the `config.cache` file. Executing `Configure` when this file exists causes cached values to be replaced again and the problem still remains.

Here is the email address of the `Configure` script maintainer: **bfriesen@simple. dallas.tx.us**.

If you are unable to find the solution, send him your `config.log` file with a brief description of the problem as follows:

**operating system type (as reported by 'uname -a') the compiler/compiler-version**

# Summary

In this chapter we learned that depending on our platform we can use a binary version of ImageMagick to install it or we can compile it personally from its source files.

On UNIX-like operating systems, sometimes the compiling process contains additional steps for other ImageMagick features and packages, which means that we have to download them from provided links, unpack them, and finally build them in our computer search/run path.

The important step in ImageMagick installation on every platform is setting the environment search/run path to the location of the ImageMagick utilities.

Finally building the program from source may encounter to some common problems and errors. The `Configure` script is a useful tool, which not only helps us to set up the program installation process but also can be used for detecting and correcting errors. If you are unable to solve the installation or configuration problems get help from supported forums and emails. In the next chapter we will study ImageMagick's utilities and interfaces.

# 3
# Convert and Mogrify

We learned from Chapter 1 that any image processing activity in ImageMagick can be done using its utilities. The `convert` utility is one that contains many parameters for implementing more than seventy percent of ImageMagick features. We can see that `mogrify` is similar to `convert` in some situations. These utilities will be studied in depth in this chapter and we will get familiar with their image processing and other capabilities.

We will concentrate on parameters and their practical usage. These are very important because we will see them being repeated for other ImageMagick utilities during the next chapters. As a matter of fact all of ImageMagick's functionality comes from about 200 options that may be used in several utilities. The question is, if the result is the same then what is the point of repeating the same options for different utilities?

Good question. In order to find out the answer we have to analyze the ImageMagick utilities' anatomy. So let's start our trip with this one: `convert`.

## Convert Syntax and Options

For running `convert` use the following scheme:

```
convert [ options ...] file [ options ...] file
```

As you can see there are some options in front of file names. These options execute our requests on files that have been specified.

Based on what option we choose tasks like format conversion, image transformation or filter application will be done. Maybe the simplest usage of this utility is something like this:

```
convert mylogo.bmp mylogo.jpg
```

In this example, the format of the specified file is converted from .bmp to .jpg. There are many options and parameters that we can use with convert so that with the help of them some complicated image processing can be done in a multi-line convert call.

In the next section, we start with a simple image and while working on it to achieve professional art work, introduce you to some great features of the convert utility.

# How to Draw Basic Shapes with Convert

Convert can be used to draw curves, lines, circles, ellipses, rectangles, polygons, texts, and even to mix two images. Although we will introduce the -draw parameters during this book, the complete list is provided in Appendix B.

This is the overall syntax of the -draw option.

```
-draw '<our shape> coordinates'
```

In this scheme instead of <our shape> we can place our desired shape keyword (that is, circle or rectangle). For example the following command will draw a black line from (10,10) to (70,90) on a white page with 80x100 dimensions and then save the result in a bitmap file:

```
convert -size 80x100 xc:white -draw 'line 10,10 70,90' line.bmp
```

As you can see with this convert command four options are used. The part of this command which draws the line is:

```
-draw 'line 10,10 70,90'
```

In which 10,10 indicates the coordinates of the start point and 70,90 indicates the end point of the line. At the beginning of this command there is a -size option, which tells ImageMagick to create a file eighty pixels wide and hundred pixels high. Next, we set the background color of our file to white with the xc:white option. There are several ways of defining colors in ImageMagick, which we shall discuss later. For now just use this option to set the white color as the background.

If we leave the xc: parameter without any color, then the file will use white as the background. By default, the background color is white and the drawing color is black.

The last step is to save our work as a graphic file. In order to do this, simply specify a file name and a graphic format extension at the end of this command. Use the display command as shown below to view the graphic file in ImageMagick:

```
display line.bmp
```

Fig 3-1: The Output of the display line.bmp Command

If you are a Windows user, you may encounter the following error while executing the above example:

**Non-conforming drawing primitive definition 'rectangle'**

In Windows you have to use "instead of" for commands. So that the example has to be changed as follows in Windows:

```
convert -size 80x100 xc:white -draw "line 10,10
70,90" line.bmp
```

In addition, the name of the program used to display images in Windows is `imdisplay.exe`. Hence, for showing the result in Windows we can use this command:

```
Imdisplay line.bmp
```

# Workshop I: Creating a Simple Logo

Let's work on something practical. Do you believe we can design logos with just the -draw option? We are going to design the Packt Publishing logo in this workshop. Take a look at the Packt logo on the cover of this book and try to guess what primitives can be used to implement it.

1. Create an empty file with a white background and name it `packt_logo.gif`.

   ```
   convert -size 300x150 xc:  packt_logo.gif
   ```

   The file `packt_logo.gif` is three hundred pixels wide and one fifty pixels high and the background color is white. Note that the `xc:` parameter is empty.

2. Draw two black vertical rectangles on the left and right sides of the image.

   ```
   convert packt_logo.gif -draw 'rectangle 0,0 40,140' -draw
   'rectangle 260,0 300,140' packt_logo.gif
   ```

   Let's examine this command. In this command, we open the previous created file, `packt_logo.gif`, draw two vertical rectangles and save the result by specifying the name at the end of the command.

Fig 3-2: Drawing Black Rectangles on Both Sides of the Image

3.  Draw a white rectangle in the middle of the image as follows.

    ```
    convert packt_logo.gif -fill white -draw 'rectangle 15,8 285,132'
    packt_logo.gif
    ```

    By default the drawing color is black. So in this command we use the `-fill`
    option to change the color to white.

Fig 3-3: Our Work after Drawing the White Rectangle

4.  Now it is time to insert some text.

    ```
    convert packt_logo.gif -fill orange -pointsize 80 -draw "text
    20,95 'PACKT'" -fill black -pointsize 27 -draw "text 68,147
    'PUBLISHING'" Packt_logo.gif
    ```

5.  For writing the word **PACKT** we have to change the color into orange. We
    can do this by calling the `-fill` option. Text size can be set by `-pointsize`
    and finally by calling:

    ```
    -draw "text <x,y -coordinates on which text will be displayed>
    'Our text' "
    ```

    the desired text will be displayed. Note the second fill command. We set
    the color to black otherwise the word **PUBLISHING** would be displayed in
    orange. Here is the completed logo:

Fig 3-4: The Final Logo

There are some differences between this logo and the original one. The word **PACKT** has to be taller and **PUBLISHING** must fill the space between the two brackets. Transformation options for this will be introduced later.

You may notice that for specifying colors we use names like red, yellow, or darkblue. The question is, if we don't like to use numbers for representing colors (as in the command-line applications) then what color names can we use in our commands? In other words what are the valid names for colors in ImageMagick? Use the following command to see the complete list:

**identify –list color**

In this workshop we design the logo in four steps but keep in mind that in ImageMagick we can write complex commands and execute multiple tasks using just one single command. For example, we can implement the above logo using a single command as follows:

```
convert -size 300x150 xc: -draw 'rectangle 0,0 40,140' -draw
'rectangle 260,0 140,300' -fill white -draw 'rectangle 15,8 285,132'
-fill orange -pointsize 80 -draw "text 20,95 'PACKT'" -fill black -
pointsize 27 -draw "text 68,147 'PUBLISHING'" Packt_logo.gif
```

# Painting Methods

One of the important roles of the -draw option is filling an area with a specified color. There are many parameters for doing this. In fact all of them use point as the basic parameter. In the next workshop we will study them in detail.

# Workshop II: Color Filling with –draw

1. Make a 400x100 .png file and draw the following items on it:

Fig 3-5: Creating an Image with the Draw Option

You know how to do this from the previous workshop, don't you? There is just one new tip. For defining and using a stoke around the text add the following code to your **convert** command call:

```
convert <required codes for page setting,color definitions &
rectangle drawings> ... -stroke white strokewidth:2 -font Tahoma
-pointsize 48 -fill black draw "text 3,70 'COLOR BOUNDARY'" color_
test.png
```

The -stroke parameter sets the color of the stroke and -strokewidth defines its thickness. Use the -font parameter to specify a font for our text.

2.  Let's start our experiments by drawing a single white pixel on our image:

```
convert color_test.png -fill white -draw 'color 7,50 point' color_
test_point.png
```

The color parameter in the -draw option indicates that we are going to paint the specified location with the color that we have set in the -fill parameter. We will see there are several methods for painting. In this example using the point parameter at the end of the -draw option we just put a single pixel on the image.

Fig 3-6: Draw a White Pixel on the Specified Coordinate (7,50)

3.  -draw has an ability to replace the current color with whichever color we specify:

```
convert color_test.png -fill orange -draw 'color 7,50 replace'
color_test_replace.png
```

Fig 3-7: All Occurrences of Black have been Replaced
with Orange using the Replace Parameter

As you can see the black color is replaced with orange wherever it is found.

4.  In the letter shapes that are curved there are some unchanged colors. We can specify a larger threshold for replacing color with the help of the `-fuzz` parameter:

```
convert color_test.png -fill darkred -fuzz 5% -draw 'color 7,50
replace' color_test_replace_with_fuzz.png
```

Fig 3-8: Using –fuzz we can Obtain a smoother Result

5.  Be careful while using the `-fuzz` parameter because specifying large values may overpaint more adjacent colors and fill greater boundaries. In the following command although we put a green pixel on the first vertical rectangle (on the left) setting a bigger value for `-fuzz` paints a larger area:

```
convert color_test.png -fill green -fuzz 40% -draw 'color 5,5
replace' color_test_replace_with_higher_fuzz.png
```

Fig 3-9: A 40% Fuzz Causes Many Colors to be Replaced –
Probably too Many in Most Cases

6.  In the previous steps we painted discrete areas. The command to be used for filling just a bounded area is shown below:

```
convert color_test.png -fill yellow -bordercolor "RGB(0,0,153)"
-draw 'color 395,95 filltoborder' color_test_fill_to_border.png
```

Fig 3-10: At the Southwest Corner the Area Surrounded by
Blue Color RGB(0,0,153) Turns to Yellow

In this command, the `-bordercolor` parameter is used for defining the boundary color of the area that should be painted with yellow. There are several ways to define color in ImageMagick. In this example we used the RGB (R, G, B) method in which each color is represented by a maximum three digit decimal number. Here is the complete method of representing colors in ImageMagick:

| Color notation | Description |
|---|---|
| Use color name itself | see the names by: identify -list |
| #RGB | R, G, and B are 4-bit hex numbers |
| #RRGGBB | R, G, and B are 8-bit hex numbers |
| #RRRGGGBBB | R, G, and B are 12-bit hex numbers |
| #RRRRGGGGBBBB | R, G, and B are 16-bit hex numbers |
| #RRGGBBAA | R, G, and B are 8-bit hex numbers and A is used for transparency |
| #RRRGGGBBBAAA | R, G, and B are 12-bit hex numbers and A is used for transparency |
| #RRRRGGGGBBBB | R, G, and B are 16-bit hex numbers and A is used for transparency |
| rgb(r,g,b) | r, g, and b are decimal numbers |
| rgb(r,g,b,a) | r, g, b, and a are decimal numbers |

7. We use the same -fuzz rules for the -bordercolor parameter:

```
convert color_test.png -fill yellow -bordercolor "RGB(0,0,153)"
-fuzz 15% -draw 'color 395,95 filltoborder' color_test_fill_to_
fuzzborder.png
```

Fig 3-11: A 15% Fuzz Causes the Border Area to be Limited

8. Finally, do you want to fill the whole image with a desired color? Then use the reset parameter in the -draw option:

```
convert color_test.png -fill lime -draw 'color 395,95 reset'
color_test_reset.png
```

Fig 3-12: Filling an Image using the Reset Parameter

# Deformations

Besides drawing and painting abilities there are some parameters that can be used for image deformations. For example with the `-implode` option we can suck or blow the pixels of an image. Here is its usage:

```
convert {input image} -implode value {output image}
```

Positive values suck the pixels and negative ones blow the pixels of the image. The option works on drawings too. See the following example:

```
convert -size 200x70 xc:darkred -fill white -draw 'roundrectangle 5,5
195,65 5,5' -fill black  -pointsize 35 -draw "text 12,45 'i m p l o d
e'"        -implode 0.5 implode.gif
```

This command first creates text on a white background with a red border (Fig 3-13a) and then implodes it by 0.5 (Fig 3-13b).

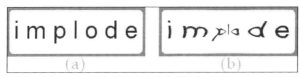

Fig 3-13: Implode Option

There is a little tip about this white background. It has rounded corners. We can draw it using the `roundrectangle` parameter:

```
-draw 'roundrectangle x0,y0 x1,y1 wc,hc'
```

Here, x and y are used for drawing coordinates and wc and hc are used for defining the horizontal and vertical radius of rounded corners. In the `-implode` option we can set the blowing status using negative values. Here is an example:

```
convert -size 200x70 xc:darkred -fill white -draw 'roundrectangle 5,5
195,65 5,5' -fill black  -pointsize 35 -draw "text 14,45 'e x p l o d
e'" -implode -3 implode.gif
```

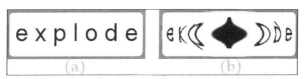

Fig 3-14: Making an Exploding Effect by using Negative Values (-3) in the -implode Option

Another deformation in ImageMagick parameters is `-swirl`. As its name shows we can use it to create spiral effects in the middle of the current image. It has only one parameter, which is used for degrees of spiral. Use positive values for counter clockwise and negative values for clockwise rotation.

The -wave option is another deformation option. It has two parameters—amplitude and wavelength. The amplitude sets the height of the wave and wavelength defines the distance between two waves.

Let's see examples for these two deformations. In these examples just the last part of the command makes the requested deformation and previous lines are used to draw two parallel rectangles:

```
convert -size 200x70 xc:darkred -fill white -draw 'roundrectangle 5,5
195,65 5,5' -fill black -draw 'rectangle 5,25 195,31' -fill red -draw
'rectangle 5,39 195,45' -swirl -360 swirl.gif
```

Fig 3-15: Make Spiral Effect Clockwise

```
convert -size 200x70 xc:darkred -fill white -draw 'roundrectangle 5,5
195,65 5,5' -fill black -draw 'rectangle 5,25 195,31' -fill red -draw
'rectangle 5,39 195,45' -wave 5x20 wave.gif
```

Fig 3-16: Making Waves with +/-5 Pixels
Height and 20 Pixels Length

Be careful while using the -wave option because every value you set for amplitude will affect the original height of the result image. For example in the previous sample although we defined a 100x70 dimension for the image after using this effect the height of the image became 80:

5x(amplitude) x 2 = 10     10 + 70x(image height) = 80

As we can see the effect of all these filters originally starts at the center of the image.

You may ask if there is any solution to affect a specific location of the image with these filters. The answer is the -region option. With this option we cannot only define the exact location where the filter is applied but we can also define an area limitation (width and height) for it. The -region format is as shown next:

```
-region widthxheight{+-}x{+-} y
```

Now let's see the -region option in action:

```
convert -size 600x70 xc:darkred -fill white -draw 'roundrectangle 5,5
595,65 5,5' -fill black -draw 'rectangle 5,25 595,31' -fill red -draw
'rectangle 5,39 595,45'
Simple_lines.jpg

convert simple_lines.jpg -region 90x70+10+0 -swirl 500 -region 90x70+95+0
-swirl 500 -region 90x70+190+0 -swirl -500 -region 120x70+280+0 -implode
1.5 -region 100x70+380+0 -implode -7 -region 100x70+490-10 -wave 10x50
complex.jpg
```

Who will believe that the simple output from the first piece of code (Fig 3-17a ) can be converted to something like Fig 3-17b?

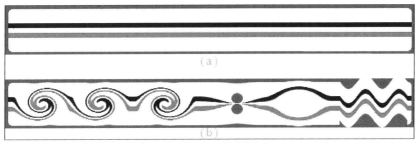

Fig 3-17: In the Second Image each Effect Corresponds to one
−region Parameter in the Second Piece of Code

One of the uses of the deformation filter is to change the appearance of portrait photos as demonstrated in the next workshop.

# Workshop III: Image Distortion

I have a portrait image and I'm going to make some changes to it with the following command. Please keep in mind you can do this on your own images but with some considerations about the coordinates that you define for the -region option.

Let's see the code and its result:

```
convert image.jpg -region 70x110+270+140 -swirl 250 -region
70x120+83+129 -swirl -250 -region 170x170+115+350 -swirl 400 -region
90x50+165+195 -implode -1 Output.jpg
```

Fig 3-18: Making Some Deformations on a Portrait

# Basic Transformations

Another important part of ImageMagick options is transformation commands. In this section we will see their syntax and usage. With these transformations we can rotate, resize, crop, change canvas, skew, flip vertically and horizontally, and roll our artworks. Let's see these commands in action.

## How to Rotate Drawings in ImageMagick

With the help of the `rotate` option we can make our desired rotation in the `convert` command. Here it is the option format:

```
-rotate deg {<}{>}
```

Use positive and negative degrees for rotating clockwise and counter-clockwise respectively.

 If you set the > operator in front of this option the rotation will be performed only if the image width exceeds the height. Use < for situations where you want the rotation to be performed on an image where its height is more than its width.

## Workshop IV: Rotating Text

1.  Write some white text on any background of your choice as shown:

```
convert back.jpg -fill white -font computerfont -pointsize 25 -
stroke blue -strokewidth 2 -draw "text 20,130 'Fantastic Rotation
!!!'" straight.jpg
```

Fig 3-19: Writing Simple Formatted Text on a Background

2.  Now we spin the text counter-clockwise by thirty degrees. This step is a little tricky. As you can see, if we use the following code then the text will stay still and the background image will be rotated as shown in Fig 3-20a.

```
convert back.jpg -fill white -rotate 30-font computerfont -
pointsize 25 -stroke blue -strokewidth 2 -draw "text 20,130
'Fantastic Rotation !!!'" r1.jpg
```

3.  The solution is to use the `rotate` parameter in the text -draw option (Fig 3-20b):

```
convert back.jpg -fill white -font computerfont -pointsize 25 -
stroke blue -strokewidth 2 -draw "rotate 30 text 20,130 'Fantastic
Rotation !!!'" r2.jpg
```

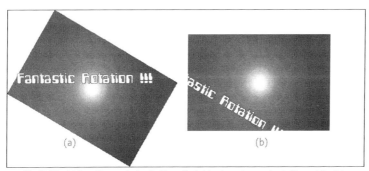

(a)                    (b)

Fig 3-20: Using the -rotate Option Outside (as shown in (a)) and Inside
(as shown in (b)) the -draw Option

When we rotate an entire scene there are always some extra triangles that will be produced to keep the image rectangular. In the command that corresponds to Fig 3-20a, if you set the background color to something other than white you will see that the triangles at the corners will be painted that color.

4. The drawback of this solution is that we have to define new coordinates for the text so that it aligns correctly in the middle of background:

```
convert back.jpg -fill white -font computerfont -pointsize 25 -
stroke blue -strokewidth 2 -draw "rotate 30 text 75,35 'Fantastic
Rotation !!!'" r2.jpg
```

Fig 3-21: Setting the Correct Rotation Coordinates

It seems that dealing with the rotation coordinates in this manner is a little complicated. Moreover, we have adjusted the text experimentally and it may not end up correctly placed, right at the center of the background. So it is better to use the -gravity option to do it precisely. Here is the format:

```
-gravity location
```

5. The gravity option uses nine locations for adjusting drawing art works on a background. You can see the names and positions of these regions in the following image.

Fig 3-22: Partitioning an Image with Gravity Values

Based on this information it is better to use following command to achieve exact aligning:

```
convert back.jpg -gravity center -fill white -font computerfont -
pointsize 25 -stroke blue -strokewidth 2 -draw "rotate 30 text 0,0
'Fantastic Rotation !!!'" precise_rotate.jpg
```

6. Now let's do it again and this time add some blur effect to the text. First we create some white text and apply the radial blur effect to it.

```
convert -size 300x240 xc:transparent -gravity center -fill
lightblue -font computerfont -pointsize 25 -draw "rotate 15 text
0,0 'Fantastic Rotation !!!'" -radial-blur 20 blur_rotate.png
```

Fig 3-23: Make a 20 degree Radial Blur on the 15 degree Rotated Text

In this command we use the -radial-blur option to make our effect. This option has a single parameter as the blur rotation degree.

 There are plans for a consolidation of some of the specialized blurs. As such -radial-blur may change to a different name and syntax.

7. Now we mix it with the background:

```
convert back.jpg -gravity center -draw 'image over 0,0 0,0 blur_
rotate.png' Final_background.jpg
```

Fig 3-24: The Radial Blurred Rotated Text is Mixed with the Background

As you can see we use the image parameter in the -draw option for mixing two images. There are some compositing methods too. We will study them in depth soon. For now we use the over method.

 Warning: ImageMagick developers are planning to revise the commands and syntax for specialized blurs. As such, -radial-blur may change its name or usage. So if this example stops working, please check the ImageMagick documentation.

8.  The last step is inserting the rotated text on the current image. So we repeat the command but this time with a 15 degree rotation.

    ```
    convert final_background.jpg -gravity center -fill white -font
    computerfont -pointsize 25 -stroke blue -strokwidth 2 -draw
    "rotate 15 text 0,0 'Fantastic Rotation !!!'" fantastic_rotate.jpg
    ```

    Look at the piece of art work you've just created.

Fig 3-25: Final Result

# How to Resize Drawings in ImageMagick

There are two options for resizing in ImageMagick. The first is the -resize option. With this option we can set a filter for adjusting resized pixels. As a matter of fact when we specify a new dimension for a drawing, it will look to its partner option, -filter to see what kind of algorithm should be used for resizing. The -filter option has several methods that are used for smooth pixel conversions. If we use the -resize option without -filter then based on the image or drawing that we are working on, the best algorithm will be select internally.

The -filter option has fifteen different parameters, which can be found in Appendix B.

The -resize parameters are as follows:

    -resize *value* {%} {@} {!} {<} {>}

You can use just a single value with this option, so if you set the width of an image its height will be resized to maintain the image aspect ratio. For example using -resize 400x on an 800x600 image will reduce its size to 400x300, and using -resize x480 on this image will produce an image with 640x480 dimensions.

For changing the image size as a percentage of the original one, use the % operator. For example using -resize 40% on an 800x600 image will produce a 320x240 image. Use an @ operator to specify the maximum area in pixels of an image.

Use < to change the dimensions of the image only if its width or height exceeds the size that you have specified and use > to change dimensions if both of its dimensions are less than the specification.

Keep in mind, the output of a resized image with the `-resize` option usually is a smoothed image. But what can we do if we were looking for a pixilated resize operation?

Another alternative to the resize task in ImageMagick is the `-sample` option. Here is the usage:

```
-sample widthxheight{+-}x{+-}y
```

The width and height specify image dimension. In the next example we will see the usage of these two resizing options.

First we draw four adjacent colored rectangles (Fig 3-26a) as follows:

```
convert -size 30x20 xc: white -fill red -draw 'rectangle 0,0 15,10'
-fill blue -draw 'rectangle 15,0 30,10' -fill green -draw 'rectangle
0,10 15,20' -fill yellow -draw 'rectangle 15,10 30,20' Rectangles.jpg
```

It will create a little image (30x20) so let's enlarge it using the options that we are already familiar with.

```
convert rectangles.jpg -resize 900% rect_resized.jpg
```

In this example using `900%` as the parameter of `-resize` will enlarge it to nine times its original size (Fig 3-26b). Now let's do it again with the `-sample` option and this time let's specify a value as the new image height (Fig 3-26c).

```
convert rectangles.jpg -sample x180 rect_resampled.jpg
```

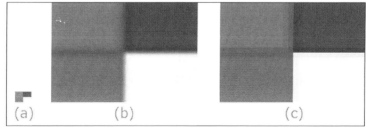

Fig 3-26: (a) Original image, (b) Enlarged with –resize, (c) Enlarged with –sample

# How to Crop Images Using ImageMagick

ImageMagick has several methods for cropping. Sometimes we want the remainder of a cropped image to be extracted and saved as a new image and sometimes we want to add a slice to the current image. In this section we will see how to handle different cropping methods.

This -crop option includes the same parameters as –sample.

```
-crop widthxheight{+-}x{+-}y{%}
```

Again width and height are used for size of cutting area and x and y are used for defining the cutting offset. It is possible to specify a percentage of original images as the cutting area with the % operator.

In the following code we cut and save a 110x70 pixels area of the specified image starting at the 60x50 coordinate:

```
convert sample.png –crop 110x70+60+50  cropped.jpg
```

Fig 3-27: Image Cropping

Be careful when you use the -crop option with .png or .gif formats. In these formats you can save image canvases and offsets too and it will produce unwanted results during cropping. So we need to remove the page info in these files by using the +repage option after –crop or using ! at the end of the crop argument as follows:

```
convert sample.png –crop 110x70+60+50 +repage  cropped.png
```

Suppose that we are going to cut the center of an image with specified width and height. One way to do it is to specify the exact area and offset for the cutting process. A better solution is to do it with help of the –gravity option. In the next example a 140x60 area will be cut from the center of an image.

```
convert temple.tif –gravity center –crop 140x60+0+0  cropped_center.jpg
```

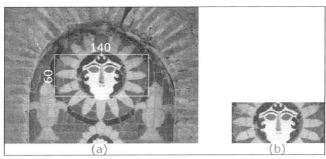

Fig 3-28: Crop from Center

# The –shave Option

In the previous example we eliminated the borders from an image and saved the result as a new image. A better method to perform this kind of image cutting is -shave. This option has following format:

```
-shave widthxheight{%}
```

It will cut borders with the values specified in the width and height parameters. In the previous example the dimension of the image 292x200 and with the following summarized command we can achieve the same result as earlier:

```
convert temple.tif –shave 76x70  shaved.jpg
```

# Inserting and Deleting Rows and Columns in Images

There is a pair of options that can be used for inserting or deleting vertical or horizontal areas on the image. The first one, -splice is used for inserting:

```
-splice widthxheight{+-}x{+-}y{%}
```

The description of x and y in this option is as before. But the width and height parameters are used for specifying the column and row size that should be inserted in the image. Here are some examples of this option's usage. Imagine the following image:

Fig 3-29: The Sample Image that we
are going to Work On

Each line of code below corresponds to part of the next image:

```
(a) convert -background gold  myimage.jpg -splice 30x20+0+0 a.jpg
(b) convert -background black myimage.jpg -splice 20x30+50+30 b.jpg
(c) convert -background red myimage.jpg -splice 20x0+30+0 c.jpg
(d) convert myimage.jpg -splice 0x20+0+40 d.jpg
```

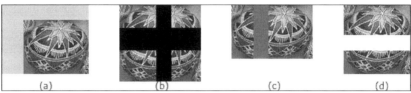

Fig 3-30: Several Insertion Methods

In the last command, no background color is defined, so -spice selects one itself.

The -chop acts in reverse; it removes the vertical or horizontal areas that are specified at a specific location.

```
-chop widthxheight{+-}x{+-}y{%}
```

# Skewing Images

For skewing images we can use the -shear option, which simply has two parameters for skewing along the x and y axes:

```
-shear X-degreesxY-degrees
```

We can even perform the skewing operation while using the -draw option with its internal parameters. We will study it in the next workshop. In that workshop a practical review of recent ImageMagcick options plus -flip and -flop is provided.

# Workshop V: The Flag

1. Create a new scene as follows and draw a skewed white rectangle on it:

   ```
   convert -size 300x200 xc:'#002377' -fill white -draw 'skewX 58
   skewY 0 rectangle -60,0 40,200' background1.tif
   ```

Fig 3-31: Using skewX and skewY for Skewing the White Rectangle

2. Create another scene with a transparent background, draw a red rectangle on it, skew it, and save it:

```
convert -size 300x40 xc:none -background transparent -fill
'#ce201a' -draw ' rectangle 0,0, 300,20' -shear 32 band.png
```

Fig 3-32: Using the -shear Option for
Skewing the Red Rectangle

3. Now mix these two file as follows:

```
convert background1.tif -draw ' image over -25,0 0,0 band.png'
background1.tif
```

Fig 3-33: The Image Parameter in the -draw Option
can be used for Mixing Drawings

 In the -draw image option, when you set the width and height of an image to zero then the original dimensions of the image will be used for drawing.

4. Crop and save an area:

```
convert background1.tif -crop 150x94+0+0 area1.tif
```

Fig 3-34: Crop to Create First Area

5.  Rotate the result 180 degree and save it in a new file:

    ```
    convert area1.tif -flip -flop area3.tif
    ```

Fig 3-35: Produce Third Area from First One

The -rotate option is not used here for 180 degree rotation. As you can see there are two new options used in this command. The -flip option is used to mirror a scene vertically and the -flop option to mirror it horizontally. Using both of them in a command gives a 180 degree rotation effect.

Neither -flip nor -flop has any parameter.

6.  Mix the previous two images as shown before:

    ```
    convert background1.tif -draw ' image over -25,-21 0,0 band.png'
    background2.tif
    ```

Fig 3-36: Mixing Drawings in Another Position

7.  Flip the whole scene horizontally:

    ```
    convert background2.tif -flop background2.tif
    ```

Fig 3-37: Mirror the Image Horizontally

8.  Crop and save a new area as follows:

    ```
    convert background2.tif -crop 150x94+150+0 area2.tif
    ```

Fig 3-38: Crop to Create Second Area

9.  Again rotate it with a -flip and -flop option:

    ```
    convert area2.tif -flip -flop area4.tif
    ```

Fig 3-39: Produce Fourth Area from the Second One

10. Now its time to arrange these four areas to achieve a new mixed scene:

    ```
    convert -size 300x188 xc:none -draw ' image over 0,0 0,0 area1.
    tif' -draw ' image over 150,0 0,0 area2.tif' -draw ' image over
    0,94 0,0 area4.tif' -draw ' image over 150,94 0,0 area3.tif'
    Mixed.tif
    ```

Fig 3-40: Mixing All Four Areas

11. For adding white and red crosses use the -splice option two times:

    ```
    convert  mixed.tif -background white -gravity center -splice 20x20
    -background '#ce201a' -splice 40x40 flag.tif
    ```

Fig 3-41: The Final Flag

# Artistic Options

For readers who are interested in the artistic capabilities of ImageMagick, this section will be wonderful. The artistic options mainly work on pixels and colors of an image so that it looks different. Most of them act on groups of pixels that are specified within a parametric radius or a specific color level.

Some of these options are discussed in the following table and the remainder will be studied during the next chapters.

| Option | Parameters | Description |
|--------|-----------|-------------|
| Charcoal | value | Converts the image to a charcoal drawing. Bigger amounts for value will produces thicker lines. |
| Edge | radius | Detect edges in an image by finding harmonic adjacent colors in the specified radius. |
| Emboss | radius | Simply emboss an image with provided radius. |
| Paint | radius | The most frequent color is identified and then the others are replaced by that and an oil paint effect produced. |
| Posterize | levels | Reduce the image colors to a limited number of color levels. |
| Shade | azimuthxheight | Convert the image to gray scale shades. The azimuth is used for setting the light source degree and height will sets the distance of light source from horizon. |
| Solarize | threshold | Will produce a negative film effect by negating all pixels above the threshold level. Setting threshold to 100 equals to using -negate option. |
| Spread | value | The value that is specified for this option acts as a radius, which is used to select a random pixel in that limit to swap with the current pixel. This effect will produce a distorted glass view. |

Due to this table the artistic options usage seems fair. Let's see them in a practical example.

# Workshop VI: Applying Various Filters on an Image

I wrote the following command for an image with 550x330 dimensions. Try it on your favorite image and see the result:

```
Convert fruits.tif  -fill white -draw "line 15,115 535,115" -draw
"line 15,215 535,215" -draw "line 125,5 125,325" -draw "line 225,5
225,325" -draw "line 325,5 325,325" -draw "line 425,5 425,325" -draw
"line 525,5 525,325" -region 99x99+26+16 -edge 25 -box "#00000050"
-gravity north -pointsize 18 -draw "text 0,0 '      edge      '" -region
99x99+226+16 -shade -30x20 -box "#00000050" -gravity north
-pointsize 18 -draw "text 0,0 '     shade     '" -region 99x99+426+16
-charcoal 1 -box "#00000050" -gravity north -pointsize 18 -draw "text
0,0 '    charcoal    '" -region 99x99+126+116 -emboss 4 -box "#00000050"
-gravity north -pointsize 18 -draw "text 0,0 '     emboss     '" -region
99x99+326+116 -solarize 95 -box "#00000050" -gravity north -pointsize
18 -draw "text 0,0 '  solarize  '" -region 99x99+26+216 -paint 9
-box "#00000050" -gravity north -pointsize 18 -draw "text 0,0 '
paint    '" -region 99x99+226+216       -spread 10 -box "#00000050"
-gravity north -pointsize18 -draw "text 0,0 '   spread   '" -region
99x99+426+216 -posterize 2  -box "#00000050" -gravity north -pointsize
18 -draw "text 0,0 '  posterize  '" Fruits_filtered.jpg
```

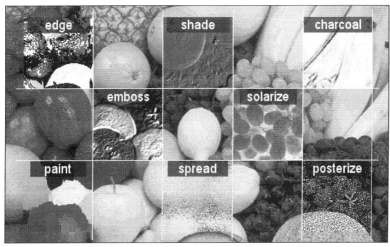

Fig 3-42: The Result of Applying Some Filters on the Image

In this code the first seven draw options draw some horizontal and vertical white lines. Then the next options affect the image state under an area specified by the —region option and write the filter name on this area.

For better view, the —box option is used here. This option will draw a bounding box under the annotating text.

You will see that sometimes while using the artistic filters you may need to try several values to get your desired result. There is an option named —preview that may speed up things for you. This option will create a montage of eight preview snapshots of the filter around the image. Here is the usage:

```
-preview type
```

The valid values for `type` are: Rotate, Shear, Roll, Hue, Saturation, Brightness, Gamma, Spiff, Dull, Grayscale, Quantize, Despeckle, ReduceNoise, Add Noise, Sharpen, Blur, Threshold, EdgeDetect, Spread, Shade, Raise, Segment, Solarize, Swirl, Implode, Wave, OilPaint, Charcoal, and JPEG.

Here are some examples for this option.

```
convert mug.jpg -preview charcoal test.jpg
```

Fig 3-43: Preview of Charcoal Effect

```
convert mug.jpg -preview implode test.jpg
```

Fig 3-44: Preview of Implode Effect

The options that we have learned in this chapter are just a small part of the whole ImageMagick options. There is still much to say about the convert utility as you will see in later chapters.

# Mogrify Syntax and Options

Mogrify uses almost the same options and the same syntax that the Convert utility but the main difference between these two utilities is:

Convert can save the image processing tasks in a new file but Mogrify overwrites them on the file that it is working on. Here is the syntax:

```
mogrify [ options ...] file
```

Another difference between these two utilities is that we can make some graphic with convert, define a canvas for it and save the result in a file whose name and format we specify but mogrify only works on existing files. It is unable to create a new file. For example if do not already have a file named line.bmp then the following command will produce an error:

```
mogrify -size 80x100 xc:white -draw 'line 10,10 70,90' line.bmp
```

The error message will say:

```
mogrify: unable to open image `line.bmp': No such file or directory.
```

But using the same parameters with convert as shown below will produce a file named line.bmp and draw a line on it:

```
convert -size 80x100 xc:white -draw 'line 10,10 70,90' line.bmp
```

So, it seems that the best uses of mogrify are processing tasks that needs no extra file production.

There is an exception for mogrify. This utility will produce new files when it is used with the -format parameter. For example when we use the following command to produce some .bmp files the original .jpg files that already exist in the directory will remain unchanged:

```
mogrify -format bmp *.jpg
```

Let's see mogrify in action and use some parameters with it in the next workshop.

# Workshop VII: The Card

In this workshop we will work on a portrait image to make an artwork similar to those found on playing cards. I choose an image with 202x196 pixels dimensions. You can choose your desired one but keep in mind it is better to select an image that when you rotate it 180 degree matches with the original one.

1.  Make a copy of your image, rotate it by 180 degrees, and name it rotated. bmp:

    ```
    Convert hafez.jpg -rotate 180  rotated.bmp
    ```

    In the above command we use convert to rotate the image because we need the original image and if mogrify is used instead then we lose the next steps.

    Another subject to notice is that we used the .bmp format to prevent loss in image quality. JPEG is a lossy format and saving the rotated image as JPEG image will affect the quality a little.

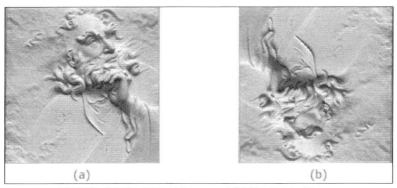

Fig 3-45: (a) The Original Image and (b) The Rotated Image

2.  Next, we expand the canvas of the original image from bottom and sides:

```
Convert -background white  Hafez.jpg -splice 40x0+0+0   -splice
40x0+242+0   -splice 0x196+0+196 -fill none -stroke black -
strokewidth 1
-draw 'rectangle 0,0 281,391 Hafez_card.bmp
```

Fig 3-46: The Expanded Canvas with the Original Image

3.  In the first part of the previous code we set the background color to white. There are three `splice` parameters. The first one adds an empty area `40` pixels wide at the left side of current image. The second `splice` parameter adds the same area at the right side of the current area and the last one will add an area with a height of `196` pixels at the bottom of the image.

We need to add a border to our work so it can be recognized from the white background of the current book page. So we set the border color to `black` in the `-stroke` option and define the border width in the `-strokewidth` option. Now we can draw a rectangle on our image that simulates the border for it and the rectangle will not fill the scene because we set the fill color to `none` in the `-fill` option.

This is not the optimum manner of implementing this step but I have introduced it just for showing the several methods available for performing a task in ImageMagick.

The better solution is to use the `-border` and `-bordercolor` options. The first one defines the border thickness and the second one will set the color for it.

```
convert hafez.jpg -splice 39x0+0+0   -splice 39x0+241+0   -splice
0x196+0+194 -bordercolor black -border1  hafez_card.bmp
```

If you observe the image carefully you will notice that the result is the same. The syntax of the `-border` command is as follows:

```
-border width x height
```

In this option we can set the width and height of the image border with the related parameters.

4.  Now place the mirrored image in the current scene using:

```
convert hafez.jpg -rotate 180 rotated.bmp
convert hafez_card.bmp -draw "image over 40,196 0,0 'rotated.bmp'"
hafez_card.bmp
```

Fig 3-47: Our Work after Placing the Rotated Part below the Original

5. Next, we have to design a name on this card:

```
convert -background white -fill black -font blackchancery
-pointsize 30 label:"H\nA\nF\nE\nZ"\ card_label.jpg
```

Fig 3-48: Card Label

6. Let's talk about the `-label` option in the previous command. With this option we can place a text label on the current image. Its syntax is as follows:

```
-label: name
```

Since we used new line characters, it will place each letter in the next line automatically.

7. Finally, we add the name at both sides of our art work:

```
mogrify -draw "image over 240,0 0,0 'card_label.jpg' -draw "rotate
180 image over -40,-391 0,0 'card_label.jpg' hafez_card.bmp
```

Fig 3-49: Inserting the Labels on the Card

At the end we used the `mogrify` command in this step. In this command we place two labels on the image simultaneously.

We used `mogrify` because there is no need to create any extra image as the product of a new task. We used the original file that the image insertion operation has been done on as the output file.

In the first option we draw the label image at the `240,0` location of the card. The second draw option is a little tricky. Because we rotate the label `180` degrees we have to use a coordinate pair that places the label exactly on the lower left corner of our image.

The negative values for location will solve this problem. The `-40` value for x position means that we want our image aligned to this location from the left (and not from the right as usual) and the `-391` value for `y` position will align the image from the bottom (not from the top as usual).

# Summary

In this chapter we learned about several aspects and usages of ImageMagick options in the Convert utility. We covered drawing primitive commands, defining color and painting methods, defining text characteristics and annotating images, various deformations and translations, and finally some artistic effects. We also covered the Mogrify command. These commands have been studied during several workshops. Although we cannot cover every single option in this book, you should now have plenty of ideas for your own experiments!

In the next chapter, another two powerful ImageMagick utilities, Composite and Montage will be studied and we will see how to use them with Convert to create complex graphics.

# 4

# Composite and Montage

For overlaying, arranging, and tiling images, the Composite and Montage utilities are very helpful.

## Composite

**The** composite utility is used for building a single image by overlaying images on top of each other. There are several modes supported by composite. In this chapter, there are some workshops that show us how to combine images with this utility. Another useful aspect of this utility is powerful masking techniques which will be studied in depth in this chapter.

The montage utility helps us to arrange images in a file without them overlapping. It means that each file has its own area and ambiences (like border, frame, and shadow). There are some options in this utility that can be used for placing images and artwork beside each other in predefined rows and columns. There are some options too that annotate the images and define frame and other ambiances for them. Workshops about montage in this chapter will show us how to do this.

## Composite Syntax and Options

For running Composite use the following scheme:

```
composite [options ...] image [[options ....] mask] image
```

The simplest way to use this utility is to type its name as a command line. This will show the valid parameters for composite as below:

```
-affine matrix          affine transform matrix
-authenticate value     decrypt image with this password
-blend geometry         blend images
```

| | |
|---|---|
| -blue-primary point | chromaticity blue primary point |
| -channel type | apply option to select image channels |
| -colors value | preferred number of colors in the image |
| -colorspace type | alternate image colorspace |
| -comment string | annotate image with comment |
| -compose operator | composite operator |
| -compress type | type of pixel compression |
| -debug events | display copious debugging information |
| -define format:option | define one or more image format options |
| -density geometry | horizontal and vertical density of the image |
| -depth value | image depth |
| -displace geometry | shift image pixels defined by displacement map |
| -display server | get image or font from this X server |
| -dispose method | GIF disposal method |
| -dissolve value | dissolve the two images a given percent |
| -dither | apply Floyd/Steinberg error diffusion to image |
| -encoding type | text encoding type |
| -endian type | endianness (MSB or LSB) of the image |
| -extract geometry | extract area from image |
| -filter type | use this filter when resizing an image |
| -font name | render text with this font |
| -geometry geometry | location of the composite image |
| -gravity type | which direction to gravitate towards |
| -green-primary point | chromaticity green primary point |
| -help | print program options |
| -interlace type | type of image interlacing scheme |
| -label name | assign a label to an image |
| -limit type value | pixel cache resource limit |
| -log format | format of debugging information |
| -matte | store matte channel if the image has one |
| -monitor | monitor progress |
| -monochrome | transform image to black and white |
| -negate | replace pixels with its complementary color |
| -page geometry | size and location of an image canvas (setting) |
| -profile filename | add ICM or IPTC information profile to image |
| -quality value | JPEG/MIFF/PNG compression level |
| -quiet | suppress all error or warning messages |
| -red-primary point | chromaticity red primary point |

```
-rotate degrees           apply Path rotation to the image
-repage geometry          size and location of an image canvas
-resize geometry          resize the image
-sampling-factor geometry  horizontal and vertical sampling factor
-scene value              image scene number
-sharpen geometry         sharpen the image
-size geometry            width and height of image
-stegano offset           hide watermark within an image
-stereo                   combine two image to create a stereo anaglyph
-strip                    strip image of all profiles and comments
-support factor           resize support: >1.0 is blurry, < 1.0 is sharp
-thumbnail geometry       create a thumbnail of the image
-tile                     repeat composite operation on image
-transform                affine transform image
-treedepth value          color tree depth
-type type                image type
-units type               the units of image resolution
-unsharp geometry         sharpen the image
-verbose                  print detailed information about the image
-version                  print version information
-virtual-pixel method     virtual pixel access method
-watermark geometry       percent brightness and saturation of watermark
-white-point point        chromaticity white point
-write filename           write images to this file
```

If you do the same with convert (enter convert as a command line without any parameters) you will discover that almost all of above options are covered in convert too. Hence the workshops in this chapter will concentrate on the composite-specific options, especially on options that simulate layer modes and mixing overlapped artworks and more importantly implementing masks.

# What is the Mask?

Before understanding the mask and its function, we have to know about the *matte* channel.

 There are at least three new technical words in the previous sentence: Mask, channel, and matte. I suppose that you have a basic knowledge about image anatomy and are familiar with color structure, channels, and so on. If that's true you will understand this chapter easily. However you can continue even without knowing this technical information.

There is an extra channel for images that have transparent features. We call this channel the matte channel. So in the previous workshops whenever we set the xc option to none, we in fact inform ImageMagick that any drawings or images in the current file will have to be placed on a transparent background.

See the following example:

```
convert -size 200x100 xc:none -fill darkslateblue -draw
"'roundrectangle' 10,10 190,65 8,8" -fill royalblue -pointsize 70
-font Times-New-Roman -stroke maroon -strokewidth 1 -draw "text 80,140
'SoSaL'" Matte_test.png
```

The output of this command is something like this:

Fig 4-1: A Simple Drawing with a Transparent Background

We set the background to transparent and hence, ImageMagick automatically creates a matte channel for our image.

 The format of this sample is *PNG*. Keep in mind currently there are only two image formats that accept the matte channel—*PNG* and *GIF*.

Let's see what a matte channel really looks like:

```
convert matte_test.png -channel matte -separate +matte
matte_channel.png
```

The -channel option is used to specify what channel we are going to be working on. The next new option in this command is -separate. This option converts a specified channel into a grayscale image. This option has no parameter.

Finally we used the +matte option to avoid writing the matte channel on output so we get a white color on empty areas. This option has no parameters to. Using -matte in commands will save an existing matte channel on the output image.

And here is the output:

Fig 4-2: Matte Channel Extracted

In this image, the areas that are white in color mean complete transparency and areas in black mean complete opaqueness.

> Black and white are not the only colors that ImageMagick uses for representing a matte channel. In fact it uses all the gray scale colors for it. The gray shades will be interpreted as semitransparent areas. So darker gray shades represent lesser transparency and lighter ones simulate more transparency.

Now after understanding the concept of the matte channel, it is time to come back to our initial question—What is the mask?

A mask image is a customized grayscale image that, when applied to a normal image, ensures that only specific areas are displayed at output.

For creating a mask image we need to make an alpha image and for making an alpha image we need to work on the matte channel.

In fact the alpha concept is a complement of the matte channel. It means that while the white color represents fully transparency in matte, it means full opaqueness in the alpha concept.

Let's see how it works.

# Workshop I: Colorful Logo

1. Select a colorful image, scale it down and resize it to the original size using the `-sample` option:

   ```
   Convert color.jpg -resize 20% -sample 500% color_new.png
   ```

   This ensures that there is no blurring or other optimization algorithms used in the `-sample` option as if this happens then the enlarged image will contain too many color squares.

Fig 4-3: Coloured Checkers Effect on an Image

2. Rotate the result by 45 degrees.

   ```
   convert color_new.png -rotate 45 color_rotated.png
   ```

3. Now crop a colorful area of the rotated image. Keep in mind that the area dimension should be match with your logo:

   ```
   convert color_rotated.png -crop 355x135+80+180  background.png
   ```

4. In this step we create our logo:

   ```
   convert -size 355x135 xc:none -fill darkred -font impact
   -pointsize 66 -draw "text 0,75 'CODE'" -pointsize 110 -draw
   "text 135,110 '2'" -pointsize 66 -draw "text 190,110 'IMAGE'"
   logo.png
   ```

5. Now make a mask image from your logo. For making the mask image, we need to extract the matte channel from the image. Then we make an alpha channel from it and finally save a mask image from the alpha channel. The alpha channel is a complement of the matte channel, so we can use the following command:

   ```
   convert logo.png -channel matte -negate -separate logo_mask.png
   ```

   In this command the `-channel matte` specifies that we are going to work on the matte channel, the `-negate` option inverts color in this channel (which corresponds to making an alpha image), the `-separate` option extracts it from the image, and finally the result is saved in the `logo_mask.png` image.

Fig 4-4: Make Mask from a Logo

6. It's time to mix the color background with the logo. In this step we use the `composite` utility.

```
composite -compose CopyOpacity logo_mask.png background.png
result.png
```

7. And here is the result:

Fig 4-5: Final Result

You've just created an excellent piece of art work. Don't you agree?

# Composite Parameters

In the last step of the previous workshop we used the `-compose` option with the `CopyOpacity` parameter, which simulates a mask for us. Beside `CopyOpacity` there are thirty-seven other parameters for `-compose`. These parameters are summarized in the following table:

| Group | Parameters |
|---|---|
| Duff-Porter | Src, Dst, Clear, Xor, Over, In, Out, Atop, Dst_Over, Dst_In, Dst_Out, Dst_Atop, |
| Mathematical | Multiply, Screen, Overlay, Bumpmap, Plus, Minus, Subtract, Difference, Exclusion |
| Channel based | CopyOpacity, CopyRed, CopyGreen, CopyBlue, CopyCyan, CopyMagenta, CopyYellow |
| Color based | Hue, Saturate, Liminize, Colorize, Lighten, Darken, ColorDodge, ColorBurn, HardLight, SoftLight |

Introducing all these parameters is beyond the scope of this book so in this chapter we will just study the Duff-Porter composite methods.

The following image can help us gain an overall understanding about the Duff-Porter composite methods:

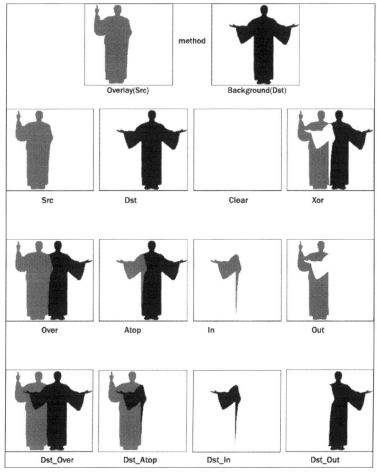

Fig 4-6: A Representation of Duff-Porter Composite Methods

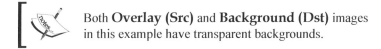

Both **Overlay (Src)** and **Background (Dst)** images in this example have transparent backgrounds.

# Workshop II: 3D Button

1. Create a transparent canvas and draw a stroked circle on it:

```
convert -size 200x200 xc:none -fill gray20 -stroke black
-strokewidth 1 -draw "circle 100,100 30,30" main_circle.png
```

Fig 4-7: A Gray Stroked Circle with a Transparent Background

2.  Create another transparent canvas and draw a khaki blurred circle on it:

```
convert -size 300x300 xc:none -fill khaki2 -draw "circle 150,150
100,100" -channel RGBA -gaussian 0x30 highlight-circle.png
```

Fig 4-8: The Highlight of our Button

3.  Mix these two circles as follow:

```
composite -compose atop -geometry -85-85 highlight-circle.png
main_circle.png button.png
```

Fig 4-9: The Basic Button

4. Flip and Flop the `button.png` and resize it:

```
convert button.png -flip -flop -resize 90% flipped.png
```

5. Now mix the result with the button:

```
composite -compose over -gravity center flipped.png button.png
button2.png
```

Fig 4-10: Mixing with Reversed Circle

6. Resize `button.png` once more and save it as a new file. This time it is not necessary to flip or flop it:

```
convert button.png -resize 80% flipped2.png
```

7. Compose it again with `button2.png`:

```
composite -compose over -gravity center flipped2.png button2.png
button3.png
```

Fig 4-11: The button after Adding the Last Part to it

8. You can insert desired text or use any transparent logo on this button:

```
convert button3.png -gravity center -fill #20202050 -pointsize
140 - font arcade -draw "text 4,20 '3D'" final_button.png
```

Fig 4-12: The Final Button with some Text on It

9. The above image is the final result obtained

# Workshop III: Fresh Candy

1. Create a 20x20 white canvas, set the background color to red, and skew it as follows:

```
convert -size 20x20 xc:white -background red -shear 45x0 band.png
```

Fig 4-13: Skewed Background

2. Create another white canvas and arrange the previous image in it:

```
convert -size 50x50 xc:white -draw "image over 0,0 0,0 band.png"
-draw "image over 40,0 0,0 band.png" -draw "image over -21,20 0,0
band.png" -draw "image over 20,20 0,0 band.png" -draw "image over
0,40 0,0 band.png" -draw "image over 40,40 0,0 band.png"  bands.tif
```

Fig 4-14: Arranging Skewed backgrounds into a New Canvas

3. Now crop the image so it can be tiled correctly:

```
convert bands.tif -crop 40x40+5+5 final-bands.tif
```

Fig 4-15: Cropping the file

A simpler command to replace steps 2 and 3 is:

```
convert band.png -roll +20+0 band.png -append -roll +10+0
bands.tif
```

4.  It is time to tile the created image on a canvas:

```
convert -size 360x80 xc:white back.png
composite -tile final-bands.tif  back.png background.png
```

Fig 4-16: Tile Option when used with Composite Tiles
an Image across the Output File Background

Again a simpler command you can use for this step is:

```
convert -size 360x80 tile:final-bands.tif background.png
```

5.  Now we create our text:

```
convert -size 360x80 xc:black -fill white -pointsize 115 -font
you're-gone -gravity center -draw "text 0,0 'CANDY'" candy.png
```

Fig 4-17: The White Text on a Black Background

6.  In this step the image will be blurred to achieve a displacement map for the next step:

```
convert candy.png –blur 0x5 candy-blur.png
```

Fig 4-18: The Blurred Text

7.  Now we apply the blurred image as a displacement map on the background:

```
composite candy-blur.png background.png -displace 4 displace.png
```

Fig 4-19: The Background after Displacement

The –displace option, moves the image pixels by the gray shades that are defined in the displacement map. Here is the –displace parameter:

```
-displace Horizontal-scale
-displace Horizontal-scale x Vertical-scale
```

With this option, white means maximum negaive displacement, mid-gray is used as a neutral displacement map and black is a maximum positive displacement.

By default, `-displace` works in both the horizontal and vertical directions. However, you can set the horizontal or vertical pixel shift manually.

8. For cutting out the extra pixels around the text we use a mask:

```
composite -compose copyopacity candy.png displace.png candy2.png
```

Fig 4-20: The Masked Area is not Clear Enough

9. As you can see the masked area is not clear enough. So we mask the blurred text and mix it with the previous image again.

```
composite -compose copyopacity candy.png candy-blur.png candy3.png
```

Fig 4-21: Mask Step

```
composite -compose darken candy2.png candy3.png candy4.png
```

Fig 4-22: Mix Step

A question for you: How can we add stroke and shadow effects to it (as follow). Try it yourself and I'll be glad to answer your questions at **sohail2d@gmail.com**.

Fig 4-23: Even More Effects

# Montage

This is another useful ImageMagick utility that is used mainly for managing a group of image thumbnails and previews. Therefore, it has become the favorite utility of users who want to create and manage photo galleries.

Besides arranging image and photo thumbnails in a page, montage can add a border, frame, label, mask and so on to an image.

## Montage Syntax and Options

For running Montage use the following scheme:

```
montage [options ...] file [ [options ...] file ...] file
```

Again, the simplest way to use this utility is to type its name in command line. This will show the valid parameters for montage as below:

```
-adjoin                  join images into a single multi-image file
-affine matrix           affine transform matrix
-annotate geometry text  annotate the image with text
-authenticate value      decrypt image with this password
-blue-primary point      chromaticity blue primary point
-blur factor             apply a filter to blur the image
-border geometry         surround image with a border of color
-bordercolor color       border color
-channel type            apply option to select image channels
-clone index             clone an image
-colors value            preferred number of colors in the image
-colorspace type         alternate image colorsapce
-comment string          annotate image with comment
-compose operator        composite operator
-compress type           type of pixel compression when writing the image
-crop geometry           preferred size and location of the cropped image
-debug events            display copious debugging information
-define format:option    define one or more image format options
-density geometry        horizontal and vertical density of the image
-depth value             image depth
-display server          query font from this X server
-dispose method          GIF disposal method
-dither                  apply Floyd/Steinberg error diffusion to image
```

| | |
|---|---|
| -draw string | annotate the image with a graphic primitive |
| -encoding type | text encoding type |
| -endian type | endianness (MSB or LSB) of the image |
| -extract geometry | extract area from image |
| -fill color | color to use when filling a graphic primitive |
| -filter type | use this filter when resizing an image |
| -flip | flip image in the vertical direction |
| -flop | flop image in the horizontal direction |
| -font name | render text with this font |
| -frame geometry | surround image with an ornamental border |
| -gamma value | level of gamma correction |
| -geometry geometry | preferred tile and border sizes |
| -gravity direction | which direction to gravitate towards |
| -green-primary point | chromaticity green primary point |
| -help | print program options |
| -interlace type | type of image interlacing scheme |
| -label name | assign a label to an image |
| -limit type value | pixel cache resource limit |
| -log format | format of debugging information |
| -matte | store matte channel if the image has one |
| -mattecolor color | frame color |
| -mode type | framing style |
| -monitor | monitor progress |
| -monochrome | transform image to black and white |
| -page geometry | size and location of an image canvas (setting) |
| -pointsize value | font point size |
| -profile filename | add, delete, or apply an image profile |
| -quality value | JPEG/MIFF/PNG compression level |
| -quiet | suppress all error or warning messages |
| -red-primary point | chromaticity red primary point |
| -repage geometry | size and location of an image canvas (operator) |
| -resize geometry | resize the image |
| -rotate degrees | apply Paeth rotation to the image |
| -sampling-factor geometry | horizontal and vertical sampling factor |
| -scenes range | image scene range |
| -set attribute value | set an image attribute |
| -shadow | add a shadow beneath a tile to simulate depth |
| -size geometry | width and height of image |

| | |
|---|---|
| `-strip` | strip image of all profiles and comments |
| `-stroke color` | color to use when stroking a graphic primitive |
| `-support factor` | resize support: > 1.0 is blurry, < 1.0 is sharp |
| `-texture filename` | name of texture to tile onto the image background |
| `-thumbnail geometry` | create a thumbnail of the image |
| `-tile geometry` | number of tiles per row and column |
| `-transform` | affine transform image |
| `-transparent color` | make this color transparent within the image |
| `-treedepth value` | color tree depth |
| `-trim` | trim image edges |
| `-type type` | image type |
| `-verbose` | print detailed information about the image |
| `-version` | print version information |
| `-virtual-pixel method` | virtual pixel access method |
| `-white-point point` | chromaticity white point |

As you can see again there are a lot of options here, many of which are the same as for the Composite utility. So based on the montage functionality we will look in depth to the options that have descriptive, arrangement, or adornment usage. These options can be summarized as follows:

| Usage | Options |
|---|---|
| Descriptive | `-label`, `-title`, `-font`, `-pointsize` |
| Adornment | `-frame`, `-shadow`, `-background`, `-fill`, `-stroke`, `-texture`, `-bordercolor`, `-mattecolor`, `-compose` |
| Arrangement | `-tile`, `-geometry`, `-mode` |

All of these usages will be studied in the next three workshops.

# Workshop IV: The Montage Descriptive Options

1. Select some of the final images from the previous workshops and use the montage utility on them as shown:

```
montage packt.png flag.png hafez.png c2i.png 3dbutton.png
candy.png montage.jpg
```

Fig 4-24: The Basic Usage of Montage

As you can see in the resulting image, these files are arranged in two rows and three columns.

2.  Add a description for each image as follows:

```
montage -label "packt" packt.png -label "flag" flag.png -label
"hafez" hafez.png -label "c2i" c2i.png -label "3dbutton"
3dbutton.png -label "candy" candy.png labeled_montage.jpg
```

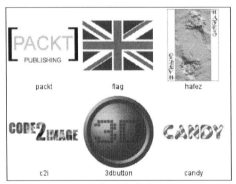

Fig 4-25: The Labeled Images

3.  It is hard to set a label for each image manually. We can use the ImageMagick format character strings instead. Given below is the complete list of format character strings:

| Character | Description |
|-----------|-------------|
| %b | file size |
| %c | comment |
| %d | directory |
| %e | filename extension |
| %f | filename |

| Character | Description |
|---|---|
| %g | page geometry |
| %h | height |
| %i | input filename |
| %k | number of unique colors |
| %l | label |
| %m | magick |
| %n | number of scenes |
| %o | output filename |
| %p | page number |
| %q | quantum depth |
| %r | image class and colorspace |
| %s | scene number |
| %t | top of filename |
| %u | unique temporary filename |
| %w | width |
| %x | x resolution |
| %y | y resolution |
| %z | image depth |
| %@ | bounding box |
| %# | signature |
| %% | a percent sign |
| %O | page offset |
| %P | page width and height |
| \n | newline |
| \r | carriage return |

For example, you can label an image with its file size as show below:

Fig 4-26: The Image Labeled with File Size

```
montage -label "%b Bytes" packt.png sized_montage.jpg
```

The advantage of this technique is that you don't need to repeat the label option for each image in the list. Instead by specifying just a set of format characters at the beginning of the command all of the consequent images in the list will obey these format characters, until the command reaches another format character string.

4.  Set the label option with the format characters as shown below and see the result:

```
montage -font tahoma -pointsize 65 -title 'My Art Works with
ImageMagick' -pointsize 10 -label 'First row\nname:%f\nsize:%b
Bytes' packt.png flag.png hafez.png -label 'Second row\nname:%f
\ndimension: %hx%w' c2i.png 3dbutton.png candy.png
labeled_montage.jpg
```

Fig 4-27: Customizing Image Labels

In the above command we first set the font to `tahoma` and font size to `65` and draw a title for the image using the `-title` option. The title will be placed at the top of the montage output. Then we reduce the font size to `10` and draw some descriptive info in the first and second row for the image labels. For the first row we have `'First row\nname:%f\nsize: %b'` as the `-label` parameter, which should be interpreted as First row, name: filename, and size: file size each one in a new line. The `\n` character inserts a new line. For the second row we have `'Second row\nname: %f\ndimension: %wx%h'`, which should be interpreted as Second row, name: file name, and dimension: file dimension.

# Workshop V: The Montage Adornment Options

1. Use the `-frame` and `–shadow` options as follows for adding frame and shadow to the montaged images:

```
montage rotate.png hafez.png -frame 5 -shadow adorn_montage1.jpg
```

Fig 4-28: Adding Frame and Shadow to Images

 The `–frame` option of the Montage utility has only one parameter and it's not necessary to define inner and outer bevels. Usually the value 5 for this option produces acceptable frames.

2. The gray color of the empty areas in previous images conflicts somehow with the inner shade of the frames. Let's do something with this color:

```
montage rotate.png hafez.png -bordercolor khaki4  -mattecolor
olive -frame 5 -shadow adorn_montage2.jpg
```

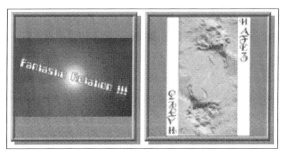

Fig 4-29: Changing the Color of the Frame border and its Background

In this command, the `–bordercolor` option is used for defining the background color of the frame and the `–mattecolor` option is used for setting the frame color itself.

We can even set the background of the entire image.

3.  Use the `-background` option to define a background color for the image:

```
montage rotate.png hafez.png -bordercolor khaki4  -mattecolor
olive -background seagreen1 -frame 5 -shadow adorn_montage3.jpg
```

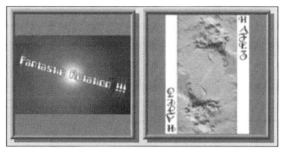

Fig 4-30: Setting the Image Background Color

4.  It is possible to set a texture image even for the background. The `-texture` option is used for this purpose:

```
montage rotate.png hafez.png   -bordercolor khaki4  -mattecolor
olive \ -texture pattern:crosshatch30 -frame 5 -shadow
adorn_montage4.jpg
```

Fig 4-31: Setting the Image Background Texture

It is not possible to use the `-background` and `-texture` options simultaneously. If you use both of them the `-texture` overrides the background setting.

The `-texture` option has one parameter that sets the background texture for an image. Here I used a built-in ImageMagick pattern. However it is possible to set an image file as the background texture. In this way that image will be tiled across the background of framed thumbnails. You can find a complete list of ImageMagick patterns in Appendix A.

This output shows that the shadow created with Montage utility is semi-transparent.

5.   Now let's add some labels and work on them:

```
montage -font arial-black -pointsize 19 -fill gold -stroke darkred
-strokewidth 1 -label '%f\nSize: %b\n Oh yes!!!\n It was a\n%wx%h
\n =< %e >= \nimage file' rotate.png hafez.png -bordercolor khaki4
-mattecolor olive -texture pattern:crosshatch30 -frame 5 -shadow
-compose overlay \adorn_montaged.jpg
```

Fig 4-32: Adding Some Text and Image Effects

This command has a lot of options. You have been introduced to line one and two of this command already. These settings simply define font, color, and size of the format characters and texts in the -label option.

The real challenge is in the -compose option. In this option we define how the image thumbnail itself should be mixed with the background color of the border. We used overlay as the parameter of -compose. That's why the final image has a shade of the background color in the thumbnails.

Try other parameters of -compose and see the result for yourself. The complete list of these values is summarized at the beginning of this chapter.

# Workshop VI: The Montage Arrangement Options

1. Set the arrangement of the image thumbnails as follows:

```
montage -label '%f' egg.png 3dbutton.png wave.png -geometry
75x75+20+10 -bordercolor orchid4 -mattecolor orchid -texture
pattern:octagons -frame 5 -shadow arr_montaged.jpg
```

Fig 4-33: Defining the Size and Distance of Image Thumbnails

Here is the `-geometry` option that specifies the size (75x75) of thumbnails and their horizontal (+20) and vertical (+10) distances from each other.

2. If we add a fourth image to the previous command we have the output arranged in two rows and two columns:

```
montage -label '%f' ring.png egg.png 3dbutton.png wave.png
-geometry 75x75+20+10 -bordercolor orchid4 -mattecolor orchid
-texture pattern:octagons -frame 5 -shadow arr_montage1.jpg
```

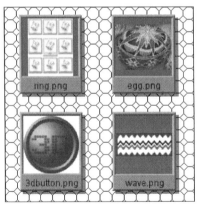

Fig 4-34: Geometry has a Limit Control on the
Arrangement of Image Thumbnails

Next, we need to learn how to custimize the placement of the thumbnails.

3. Set all of thumbnails in one row with the `-tile` option as shown below:

```
montage -label '%f' ring.png egg.png 3dbutton.png wave.png -tile
4x1 -geometry 75x75+20+10  -bordercolor orchid4   -mattecolor
orchid -texture pattern:octagons -frame 5 -shadow arr_montage3.jpg
```

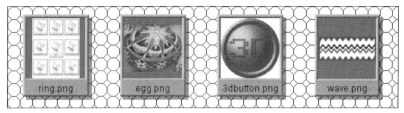

Fig 4-35: Using the −tile Option for Setting the Image Thumbnail Arrangement

The −tile option has four parameters that define the number of columns, rows, x offset, and y offset:

```
-tile column(s)x row(s) +- x +- y
```

If you set a value for the x or y parameters of the −tile option, this value will be added to (or subtracted from) the correspond parameters of the −geometry option and the final result.

4.  Add the position offsets in −tile and -geometry as follows:

```
montage -label '%f' ring.png egg.png 3dbutton.png wave.png
\-tile 4x1+15+5 -geometry 75x75+20+5  -bordercolor orchid4
-mattecolor orchid \-texture pattern:octagons -frame 5
-shadow arr_montage4.jpg
```

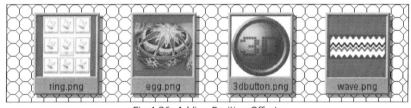

Fig 4-36: Adding Position Offsets

 If you use more than one −tile or −geometry options in one command, only the last option parameters will be approved.

5.  For controlling the image size further use the > operator with -geometry:

```
montage -label '%wx%h' ring.png egg.png redband.png boundary.png
wave.png  \-tile 5x -geometry '70x50+15+5>'  -bordercolor orchid4
-mattecolor orchid \-texture pattern:octagons -frame 5 -shadow
arr_montage5.jpg
```

Fig 4-37: Controlling Image Sizes

You see the center image has 40x40 dimensions but it is not enlarged to cover the frame. Use > for preventing images being enlarged.

> The -tile 5x means that we need a five column arrangement for images and that the number of rows is not important. Similarly, we can use -tile x3 if we need to set rows to three and the number of columns is not important.

6. You can set empty places in the montage image with the null option as follows:

```
montage -label '%wx%h' ring.png null: egg.png null: redband.png
\null: boundary.png null: wave.png null: \-tile 5x2 -geometry
"80x60+10+10>"  -bordercolor orchid4  -mattecolor orchid \-texture
pattern:octagons -frame 5 -shadow arr_montage6.jpg
```

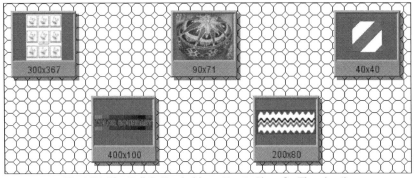

Fig 4-38: The Null Option holds an Empty Place for Thumbnails

7. Another way of arranging thumbnails is to remove the space between images by calling the -mode option:

```
montage packt.png egg.png candy.png redband.png  wave.png
-mode concatenate -tile 2x -bordercolor lightgoldenrod
-mattecolor darkgoldenrod -texture pattern:fishscales -frame
5 arr_montage7.jpg
```

Fig 4-39: Concatenating Thumbnails Together

We have not set the geometry option in this command so the original size of the images is used. The mode option is used for concatenating images:

```
-mode value
```

The value can take one of these parameters:

- **Concatenate**: For joining images without extra spaces between them
- **Frame**: For using a thicker frame on images (the frame option should not be used with this parameter)
- **Unframe**: For using bare images without frames

# Workshop VII: Creating an Indexed Image Web Page

One of the great usages of Montage is for creating HTML pages that contains the image thumbnails of all images in a directory. It is very easy:

```
montage -label '%f\n%wx%h\n%b bytes' '*.png' -tile 4x -frame 5
-shadow -geometry 80x60+10+10  -bordercolor lightgoldenrod
-mattecolor darkgoldenrod -texture pattern:verticalbricks
myphotogallery.htm
```

As you may notice there is an .htm file specified as output. Hence, this command will produce an .htm page that contains thumbnails of .png files that exist in the current directory.

If you click on each thumbnail, its full size image will be displayed in your web browser.

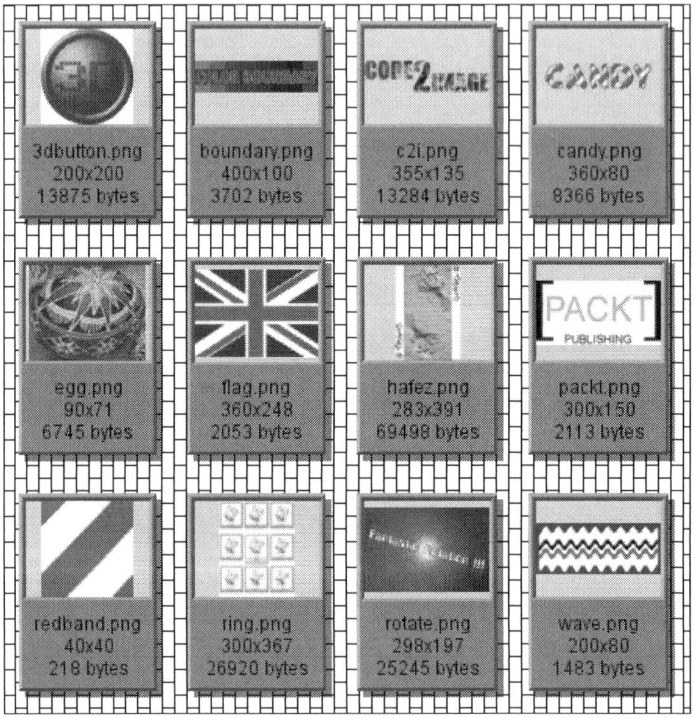

Fig 4-40: This is an HTML Page containing Image Thumbnails

In fact this command has three output files:

- **myphotogallery.gif**: The montage of all thumbnails of the images
- **myphotogallery.shtml**: An 'image map' file for the GIF image
- **myphotogallery.htm**: The HTML thumbnail index page for browsers

# Summary

The first part of this chapter showed us the power of the `composite` utility and its ability to mix multiple images or artwork in a single file. We learned how to create mask images from matte and alpha channels. Moreover we saw that the `-compose` option has about forty mixing methods that are categorized in four groups. Some of these options are discussed in this chapter's workshops.

In the second part of this chapter we studied the `montage` utility and we leaned about its thumbnailing techniques and learned how to create a photo gallery web page.

# 5

# Identify, Display, and Import

In this chapter we will see some ImageMagick utilities that are a little different from the ones we have already studied. On the other hand, by referring to the previous workshops you'll see there is always at least one image processing function that has been performed during those workshops. We used convert, mogrify, compose, and montage for tasks like:

- Creating a new canvas
- Drawing images and shapes, and inserting text
- Format conversion
- Mixing and combining files and drawings together
- Arranging files with customized settings in a new image file

The utilities that will be introduced in this chapter are different because their main task is input/output file management, and retrieving detailed info about images and ImageMagick environmental settings.

In this chapter we will see how to use display for showing the result of any image processing on an X window and we will see how to capture image data from a part of the screen or a window with the help of import. Let's start with identify and learn how to retrieve useful information about images with this utility.

## Identify

Identify is one of the special utilities in ImageMagick because, unlike other utilities, it works on image characteristics and specifications. There is a lot of helpful information that identify can retrieve from an image and display at the command line.

Beside image characteristics it can find out if an image is corrupted and report it. Moreover there is an option named -list (which can be found in other utilities as well) that helps us to find out more information about the ImageMagick software installed on our machine.

# Identify Syntax and Options

For running `identify` use the following scheme:

```
identify [options ...] image[ [options ...] file ... ]
```

The simplest way to get a list of `identify` options is typing **identify** at the command line (without any parameters):

| | |
|---|---|
| -authenticate value | decrypt image with this password |
| -channel type | apply option to select image channels |
| -crop geometry | cut out a rectangular region of the image |
| -debug events | display copious debugging information |
| -define format:option | define one or more image format options |
| -density geometry | horizontal and vertical density of the image |
| -depth value | image depth |
| -extract geometry | extract area from image |
| -format "string" | output formatted image characteristics |
| -fuzz distance | colors within this distance are considered equal |
| -help | print program options |
| -interlace type | type of image interlacing scheme |
| -limit type value | pixel cache resource limit |
| -list type | Color, Configure, Delegate, Format, Magic, Module, Resource, or Type |
| -log format | format of debugging information |
| -matte | store matte channel if the image has one |
| -monitor | monitor progress |
| -ping | efficiently determine image attributes |
| -quiet | suppress all error or warning messages |
| -sampling-factor geometry | horizontal and vertical sampling factor |
| -set attribute value | set an image attribute |
| -size geometry | width and height of image |
| -strip | strip image of all profiles and comments |
| -units type | the units of image resolution |
| -verbose | print detailed information about the image |
| -version | print version information |
| -virtual-pixel method | virtual pixel access method |

As you see the options of this utility are definitely less than those of other ImageMagick utilities. Hence, it seems that this one has been optimized just for informative purposes.

# How to Extract Information from an Image

In general, with `identify`, we can get image characteristics and attributes in three ways:

- Retrieve the brief and useful image attributes
- Retrieve the full image attributes
- Retrieve the customized image attributes

# How to get Brief Information from Images

The `-ping` option is used for getting the most efficient data. This option has no parameter and you can call it before image file name.

Based on the image format the output of this option is different. It may return image number, file name, the width and the height, whether it is color indexed (PseudoClass) or not (DirectClass), the number of colors in the image, the size of the image, its format, and the elapsed time to process the image characteristics.

 If the image is corrupted it will be reported at the command line.

Here is the brief output information of some image formats:

```
identify -ping image.png
```
*Output*: **image.png PNG 340x90 340x90+0+0 DirectClass 6kb 0.016u 0:01**

```
identify -ping image.psd
```
*Output*: **image.psd PSD 440x189 PseudoClass 256c 36kb**

```
identify -ping image.jpg
```
*Output*: **image.jpg JPEG 340x90 DirectClass 8kb 0.000u 0:01**

```
identify -ping image.tif
```
*Output*: **image.tif TIFF 300x90 DirectClass 106kb 0.000u 0:01**

```
identify -ping frame.gif
```
*Output*: **frame.gif GIF 600x420 200x200+0+0 PseudoClass 32c 44kb**

```
identify -ping image.gif
```
*Output*:
**image.gif[0] GIF 200x200 200x200+0+0 PseudoClass 2c 21kb**
**image.gif[1] GIF 200x200 200x200+0+0 PseudoClass 256c 21kb**
**image.gif[2] GIF 200x200 200x200+0+0 PseudoClass 64c 21kb**
**image.gif[3] GIF 200x200 200x200+10+0 PseudoClass 64c 21kb**
**image.gif[4] GIF 200x200 200x200+20+0 PseudoClass 64c 21kb**

```
identify -ping image.pcx
```
*Output*: **image.pcx PCX 200x200 PseudoClass 2c 1kb**

```
identify -ping image.bmp
```
*Output*: **image.bmp BMP 200x200 PseudoClass 2c 6kb**

```
identify -ping vid.mpg
```
*Output*:
**vid.mpg=>magick-amng4fao0.ppm[0] MPEG 200x200 DirectClass 117kb 0.391u 0:06**
**vid.mpg=>magick-amng4fao1.ppm[1] MPEG 200x200 DirectClass 117kb 0.391u 0:06**
**vid.mpg=>magick-amng4fao2.ppm[2] MPEG 200x200 DirectClass 117kb 0.391u 0:06**
**vid.mpg=>magick-amng4fao3.ppm[3] MPEG 200x200 DirectClass 117kb 0.391u 0:06**
**vid.mpg=>magick-amng4fao4.ppm[4] MPEG 200x200 DirectClass 117kb 0.391u 0:06**
**vid.mpg=>magick-amng4fao5.ppm[5] MPEG 200x200 DirectClass 117kb 0.391u 0:06**

```
identify -ping image.tga
```
*Output*: **image.tga TGA 100x100 PseudoClass 256c 10kb**

```
identify -ping image.ps
```
*Output*:
**identify: '%s': %s "" -q -dBATCH -dSAFER -dMaxBitmap=500000000 -dNOPAUSE -dAlignToPixels=0 "-sDEVICE=pnmraw" -dTextAlphaBits=4 -dGraphicsAlphaBits=4 "-g100x100" "-r72x72" "-sOutputFile= \magick-711iq1q" "-f \magick-t41uf93b" "-f1 image.ps".identify: `%s': %s "" -q -dBATCH -dSAFER -dMaxBitmap=500000000 -dNOPAUSE -dAlignToPixels=0 "-sDEVICE=pnmraw" -dTextAlphaBits=4 -dGraphicsAlphaBits=4 "-g100x100" "-r72x72" "-sOutputFile= \magick-g711iq1q" "-f \magick-t41uf93b" "-fimage.ps" -c showpage.**

**identify: no decode delegate for this image format ` image.ps'.**

If you specify an incorrect image format, you'll receive an output error message as follows:

```
identify -ping book.doc
```
*Output*: **identify: Improper image header 'book.doc'.**

We even can use the identify option without the –ping parameter to get some information about an image. For some formats there is no difference between using and not using the –ping option. In fact, identify with –ping attempts to read the minimal amount of the image file data needed to report.

# How to get Detailed Information from Images

The identify option for extracting full image attributes from the file is -verbose.

It will retrieve everything about an image: information like file name, dimension, size, time to process, color type, color space, channel depth, channel stats, number of colors, resolution, interlace type, background/border/matte color, page geometry, dispose method, iteration (for animated formats), compression type, orientation, signature, version, and much more.

For example, here is the output for an image in the .png format:

```
identify -verbose image.png
```

*Output*:

```
image.png PNG 200x200 200x200+0+0 DirectClass 116kb 0.000u 0:01
Image: 1.png
  Format: PNG (Portable Network Graphics)
  Geometry: 200x200
  Class: DirectClass
  Type: TrueColor
  Endianess: Undefined
  Colorspace: RGB
  Channel depth:
    Red: 16-bits
    Green: 16-bits
    Blue: 16-bits
    Alpha: 1-bits
  Channel statistics:
    Red:
      Min: 0 (0)
      Max: 58274 (0.889204)
      Mean: 22818.2 (0.348184)
      Standard deviation: 18170.2 (0.27726)
    Green:
      Min: 0 (0)
      Max: 56342 (0.859724)
      Mean: 22272.5 (0.339857)
      Standard deviation: 17552.1 (0.267828)
```

```
  Blue:
    Min: 0 (0)
    Max: 32913 (0.50222)
    Mean: 15655.8 (0.238893)
    Standard deviation: 10296.4 (0.157113)
   Alpha:
    Min: 65535 (1)
    Max: 65535 (1)
    Mean: 65535 (1)
    Standard deviation: 0 (0)
Colors: 8270
Rendering-intent: Undefined
Resolution: 72x72
Units: Undefined
Filesize: 116kb
Interlace: None
Background Color: white
Border Color: #DFDFDFDFDFDF0000
Matte Color: grey74
Page geometry: 200x200+0+0
Dispose: Undefined
Iterations: 0
Compression: Zip
Orientation: Undefined
Signature: 2c56431331bf9c1b50be1b20984f3418bbcee3946e9c88b623aa48a
3917bcdd7
Tainted: False
Version: ImageMagick 6.2.5 10/01/05 Q16 http://www.imagemagick.org
```

# How to get Customized Information from Images

The -format option is the tool that we need to extract customized information that we want. The parameter of this option is an ImageMagick format string. You can find the complete list of these control characters in the previous chapter.

Let's see some examples.

```
identify -format "Dimension: %wx%h\nFilename: %f\nFile size:%b
byte(s)" image.png
```
*Output*:
```
Dimension: 200x200
Filename: image.png
File size:118611 byte(s)
```

```
identify -format "Scene Number:%s\nDimension: %wx%h\nFilename: %f\
nFile size:%b byte(s) \nNumber of the scene(s):%n\n\n" image.gif
```

*Output*:
```
Scene Number:0
Dimension: 200x200
Filename: image.gif
File size:21568 byte(s)
Number of the scene(s):5

Scene Number:1
Dimension: 200x200
Filename: image.gif
File size:21568 byte(s)
Number of the scene(s):5

Scene Number:2
Dimension: 200x200
Filename: image.gif
File size:21568 byte(s)
Number of the scene(s):5

Scene Number:3
Dimension: 200x200
Filename: image.gif
File size:21568 byte(s)
Number of the scene(s):5

Scene Number:4
Dimension: 200x200
Filename: image.gif
File size:21568 byte(s)
Number of the scene(s):5
```

# How to Get Information about ImageMagick

During examples provided in this book you may notice that sometimes we use special names for colors, fonts, backgrounds, etc.

For example we use the name DarkSalmon as the parameter of the -fill option in the following command (instead specifying a color code) and set the -font option to fantasy:

```
convert size 100x100 xc:black -fill DarkSalmon -font fantasy draw
"text 10,50 'Hi!!!'" test.jpg
```

The question is where these reserved names come from and how to obtain a complete list of them?

There is an option in ImageMagick that is also listed in the `identify` utility. It is `-list` and it can list ImageMagick keywords based on input parameter.

For example to get the all formats supported in your ImageMagick copy enter the following command:

```
identify -list format
```

Here are the valid values for its parameters and their function:

| Parameter | Output |
| --- | --- |
| Coder | Lists the ImageMagick code names for various file formats as in coder.xml |
| Color | Lists all the color keywords and their RGB values in ImageMagick |
| Delegate | Lists all format delegates that are currently installed in ImageMagick |
| Format | Lists all formats that are currently supported in ImageMagick |
| Magic | Lists all magic codes that correspond to ImageMagick file formats |
| Module | Lists all external functions and modules installed on ImageMagick |
| Resource | Lists all memory spaces allocated for ImageMagick on you computer |
| Type | Lists all fonts that currently can be used in your commands |

# Display

The `display` utility is the basic ImageMagick program for showing images or image sequences (like all the `.png` files in a directory) on a X server.

So it works only on X servers and if you run it on Windows the following error message box will be displayed:

Fig 5-1: The Error Message when Windows is not
Running an X Window Server such as Xwin32

For ImageMagick users running Windows there is a corresponding utility called imdisplay.exe. However this is a contributed application and was not developed by the ImageMagick development team. So it does not have the capability to receive command-line options and parameters for showing images.

# Display Syntax and Options

For running display use the following scheme:

```
display  [options ...] image
```

Type display at the command line (without any parameters) and you'll get the options that you can use with this utility:

| | |
|---|---|
| -antialias | remove pixel-aliasing |
| -authenticate value | decrypt image with this password |
| -backdrop | background color |
| -background color | background color |
| -border geometry | surround image with a border of color |
| -bordercolor color | border color |
| -channel type | apply option to select image channels |
| -clip | clip along the first path from the 8BIM profile |
| -clip-path id | clip along a named path from the 8BIM profile |
| -coalesce | merge a sequence of images |
| -colormap type | shared or private |
| -colors value | preferred number of colors in the image |
| -colorspace type | alternate image colorspace |
| -comment string | annotate image with comment |
| -compress type | type of pixel compression when writing the image |
| -contrast | enhance or reduce the image contrast |
| -debug events | display copious debugging information |
| -define format:option | define one or more image format options |
| -delay value | display the next image after pausing |
| -density geometry | horizontal and vertical density of the image |
| -depth value | image depth |
| -despeckle | reduce the speckles within an image |
| -display server | get image or font from this X server |
| -dispose method | GIF disposal method |

```
-dither                      apply Floyd/Steinberg error diffusion to image
-edge radius                 apply a filter to detect edges in the image
-endian type                 endianness (MSB or LSB) of the image
-enhance                     apply a digital filter to enhance a noisy image
-extract geometry            extract area from image
-filter type                 use this filter when resizing an image
-flatten                     flatten a sequence of images
-flip                        flip image in the vertical direction
-flop                        flop image in the horizontal direction
-frame geometry              surround image with an ornamental border
-gamma value                 level of gamma correction
-geometry geometry           perferred size or location of the image
-help                        print program options
-immutable type              prohibit image edit
-interlace type              type of image interlacing scheme
-label name                  assign a label to an image
-limit type value            pixel cache resource limit
-log format                  format of debugging information
-map filename                transform image colors to match this set of colors
-matte                       store matte channel if the image has one
-mattecolor color            frame color
-monitor                     monitor progress
-monochrome                  transform image to black and white
-negate                      replace every pixel with its complementary color
-page geometry               size and location of an image canvas (setting)
-profile filename            add, delete, or apply an image profile
-quiet                       suppress all error or warning messages
-raise value                 lighten/darken image edges to create a 3-D effect
-remote                      execute a command in an remote display process
-resize geometry             resize the image
-roll geometry               roll an image vertically or horizontally
-rotate degrees              apply Paeth rotation to the image
-sample geometry             scale image with pixel sampling
-sampling-factor geometry    horizontal and vertical sampling factor
-scene value                 image scene number
-segment values              segment an image
-set attribute value         set an image attribute
-sharpen geometry            sharpen the image
```

| | |
|---|---|
| -size geometry | width and height of image |
| -strip | strip image of all profiles and comments |
| -support factor | resize support: > 1.0 is blurry, < 1.0 is sharp |
| -trim | trim image edges |
| -update seconds | detect when image file is modified and redisplay |
| -verbose | print detailed information about the image |
| -version | print version information |
| -virtual-pixel method | virtual pixel access method |
| -visual | display image using this visual type |
| -window id | display image to background of this window |
| -window group id | exit program when this window ids destroyed |

# Workshop I: Looking at Some Display Examples

As you may note, this list of parameters is a subset of those of other popular ImageMagick utilities like convert or compose. However these options act differently when used with display.

For example in the convert utility we use the -size option for defining the canvas size of the drawing or image dimensions. But in the following command this option is used for defining the window size on which the specified image should be tiled:

```
display -size 800x600 -window root wood_tile.bmp
```

The -window option in this example defines the window where the file will be placed as its background.

You can find positioning and addressing options in the display option list. This means that with display we can specify in which window we are going to display an image and what the preferred size of this window is and where the image must be displayed in it.

Look at the following example (suppose the image nature.jpg has dimensions of 640x480):

```
display -geometry 200x100 -depth 8 nature.jpg
```

This tells ImageMagick to create an X window 200 pixels wide and 100 pixels high. These dimensions are smaller than the image size so unlike with the geometry function in other utilities here we will get horizontal and vertical scroll panes to move around the image in that window.

The `-geometry` option here will not resize the image (as in the `montage` utility) or crop the out-of-view pixels (as in the `convert`, `composite`, and `mogrify` utilities).

The simplest usage of `display` is calling it to show an image:

```
display myimage.tif
```

In this form of call there is no need to use any extra option and the file will be displayed in a window. But keep in mind not all ImageMagick file formats will work in this manner.

For example `.pov` is a scripting format, which contains codes and values that should be rendered before being displayed and if you use `display` for showing this format:

```
display myimage.pov
```

You'll receive the following error message:

```
Creating vista buffer.
Creating light buffers.
File Init Error:
Attempt to malloc zero size block (File: png_pov.cpp Line: 674).

display: Delegate failed '"povray" "+i"%i"" +o"%o" +fn%q +w%w +h%h +a -q9
-kfi"%s" -kff"%n"'.
```

For showing these kinds of files, `display` needs to know the image size. So we have to use `display` as follows:

```
display -size 500x330 myimage.pov
```

Sometimes we need to study an error more precisely to find out the reason of a utility malfunction. With the `-debug` option we can create a plain text file that contains the error codes and other useful description that will help us to understand the reason for the error.

Usually most errors rise from the X11 system and display. So if you encountered an error, first try the following command:

```
display –debug x11 myimage.jpg
```

The `-debug` option has the following format:

```
-debug event
```

We can specify one or more events (separated with commas) to be logged for error detection. Here is the list of valid events for debug:

```
Annotate, Blob, Cache, Coder, Configure, Deprecate, Exception, Locale,
Render, Resource, TemporaryFile, Transform, X11, or User
```

Besides these you can use `None`, `All`, and `Trace` with this option too.

 The `User` domain is empty by default, and only the ImageMagick developers team can log the user domain in their special ImageMagick copy.

After debugging an error with this option and creating a text file, send the error link (or text file) to the ImageMagick support section at `http://www.imagemagick.org`. Or drop a message at their support forum, `http://studio.imagemagick.org/ discussion server/index.php`.

# Import

The `import` utility acts as a screen capture program. We can define an area or an entire X window screen to be captured by `import`. The data captured by `import` will be saved as an image file.

This utility will not function under the Windows platform. It works only on X servers and captures only X windows.

# Import Syntax and Options

For running `import` use the following scheme:

```
import [options ...] image
```

Typing `import` at the command line (without any parameters) will show the options that may be used with this utility:

```
-adjoin                joins images into a single multi-image file
-annotate geometry text  annotate the image with text
-border                include image borders in the output image
-channel type          apply option to select image channels
-colors value          preferred number of colors in the image
-colorspace type       alternate image colorspace
-comment string        annotate image with comment
-compress type         type of pixel compression when writing the image
-contrast              enhance or reduce the image contrast
```

| | |
|---|---|
| -crop | geometry preferred size and location of the cropped image |
| -debug events | display copious debugging information |
| -define format:option | define one or more image format options |
| -delay value | display the next image after pausing |
| -density geometry | horizontal and vertical density of the image |
| -depth value | image depth |
| -descend | obtain image by descending window hierarchy |
| -display server | get image or font from this X server |
| -dispose method | GIF disposal method |
| -dither | apply Floyd/Steinberg error diffusion to image |
| -encoding type | text encoding type |
| -endian type | endianness (MSB or LSB) of the image |
| -frame | include window manager frame |
| -geometry geometry | perferred size or location of the image |
| -gravity   type | horizontal and vertical text placement |
| -help | print program options |
| -interlace type | type of image interlacing scheme |
| -label name | assign a label to an image |
| -limit type value | pixel cache resource limit |
| -log format | format of debugging information |
| -monitor | monitor progress |
| -monochrome | transform image to black and white |
| -negate | replace every pixel with its complementary color |
| -page geometry | size and location of an image canvas (setting) |
| -quality   value | JPEG?MIFF?PNG compression level |
| -quiet | suppress all error or warning messages |
| -repage   geometry | size and location of an image canvas |
| -resize geometry | resize the image |
| -rotate degrees | apply Paeth rotation to the image |
| -sampling-factor geometry | horizontal and vertical sampling factor |
| -scene value | image scene number |
| -screen value | select image from root window |
| -set attribute value | set an image attribute |
| -sharpen geometry | sharpen the image |
| -silent | operate silently i.e. don't ring any bells |
| -strip | strip image of all profiles and comments |
| -support factor | resize support: > 1.0 is blurry, < 1.0 is sharp |
| -trim | trim image edges |
| -type   type | image type |
| -verbose | print detailed information about the image |
| -version | print version information |
| -virtual-pixel method | virtual pixel access method |
| -window id | display image to background of this window |

# Workshop II: Looking at Some Import Examples

To capture the entire X server screen and save it as a black and white `.gif` file use the following command:

```
import -window root -monochrome x.gif
```

For capturing the area from (10,20) to (190,169) from a window with ID `0x024001c` and saving the result in a `.jpg` file use the following command:

```
import -window 0x024002c -geometry 180x149+10+20 area_captur1.jpg
```

For capturing an image from a window and including the window frame itself in the saved image use the following command:

```
import -window 0x024003b -frame area_captured2.jpg
```

For capturing an image from a window and placing some text at the center of the captured image use the following command:

```
import -window 0x024001b -gravity center -annotate 'ImageMagick' area_
captured3.jpg
```

For saving a captured image (from any window that you specified) as an eight-bit color image use the following command:

```
import -window root -depth 8 area_captured4.jpg
```

For saving a captured image (from any window that you specified) with some commentary description use the following command:

```
import -window root -comment 'this file is captured with ImageMagick
Import utility' area_captured4.jpg
```

The image comments can be accessed by using the `%c` character format string. For example the following command will produce an image thumbnail with a 5-pixel frame and shadow and annotate it with the phrase that was inserted into it as a comment using the import utility:

```
montage area_captured4.jpg -label "%c" -frame
5 -shadow montaged.jpg
```

# Summary

In this chapter we have studied three new ImageMagick utilities:

- `identify`: Suitable for getting more information about images
- `display`: Used for showing an image on X window systems
- `import`: Used for grabbing a selected area or entire X window screen and saving the output as an image file

We are now familiar with the `-list` option too, which is used to extract information about ImageMagick keywords and installed features.

In the next chapter we will learn about animation techniques in ImageMagick.

# 6
# Animation

This chapter deals with animation in ImageMagick. There are two ways of handling an animation. We can just show a number of still images in a directory with a predefined delay or we can make an animated file with them and show the result. The convert and display utilities are capable of making and showing animated files. Beside these utilities animate is specially developed for working on animations in ImageMagick.

In this chapter we will study animate, its weaknesses and strengths, and then during some workshops we will use convert to make some animated files.

## Animate Syntax and Options

For running the animate utility, use the following scheme:

```
animate [ options ...] file
```

We can use the display options for animate as their options are almost the same. The simplest usage of animate is as follows:

```
animate myimage.gif
```

This command simply shows the animated frames stored in the myimage.gif file.

```
animate *.tif
```

This one will continuously show all the .tif files in the current directory.

The important note to Windows users is that the animate utility is a X server utility so it cannot be executed on Windows. If you type animate at the command line and press enter you will be encountered an error message box as in Fig 6-1. This is one of the drawbacks of animate.

Fig 6-1: Animate is a X Server Application

# How to Display an Animation

Animate has a configuration file that sets up the manner of playing animated files. The main settings of this file are:

    AnimateColor color

This line defines the color of the window outline in which the animated file is going to be played.

    AnimateDelay msecs

The frame rate (number of displayed frames per second) of the animation is defined by this line. The msecs value sets the delay between frames of the animation in milliseconds.

    AnimateIterations iterations

This line tells animate the number of iterations of the animated frames. Setting this parameter to zero will repeat the animation for ever.

    AnimateWidth width

The line thickness is defined by this line. Lower values will produce fast thin lines.

    AnimateResize mode

Transformations like zoom, zoom3D, twist, flip, turn & random are defined by this setting.

After setting up these values, the animate utility is executed based on them. This means that if you need to run an animated file with higher frame rate than before, you have to change the AnimatedDelay parameter of the configuration file and save the changes and then run your animated file.

Another drawback of this utility is the limit of execution. We can run only one animation at a time so if we want to execute another animation we have to first terminate the previous process.

# How to Create an Animation

As I mentioned before, the `animate` utility just shows animated files. So the best way of creating animation files is the `convert` utility. The easiest manner of making an animation with `convert` is to join the still images in a directory (which have the same format) and save them as an animated format like `.gif`, `.mpg`, `.m2v`, or `.mnv`.

```
convert *.jpg animated.mpg
```

This command places all the `.jpg` files in the current directory (in alphabetical order) as frames of an animated `.mpg` file. If you play the `.mpg` file, the frames will show rapidly and the animation will loop from the start. Using the above command, the dimensions of the animated `.mpg` file that is created is based on the first image page size and all the other `.jpg` files will be aligned to the upper left corner of the created canvas.

Questions like what happens if the `.jpg` files have various dimensions, how will the small images align to the animation frame, how to slow down the play-back and issues like play-back control and creating more complicated animated files are the subjects of the next workshops. Before starting we need to know some options that are required for these workshops. There are three main options that `convert` needs for creating animated GIFs:

- `-delay ticks`: The value specified in the `ticks` parameter defines how long the next frame should wait to be displayed. Each tick is equivalent to 1/100 second.

- `-dispose method`: For GIF animations, this option sets the disposal method between frames. The four parameters available for this option are:
  - `undefined`: No disposal specified.
  - `none`: The next frame will be displayed on the content of current frame, which will not be disposed of between frames.
  - `background`: Before displaying the next frame the image area will be filled with the background color.
  - `previous`: Overwrites the image area with what was there prior to rendering the image.

- `-loop iterations`: This specifies the number of times the animation repeats is set using the `loop` option. For infinite iteration we have to use zero as its value.

So let's start creating animations using these options.

# Workshop I: Simple Type Effect

In this workshop we will see how to create animations that every frame may overlaid on current contents of image.

Create seven `.gif` images, each of which contains a letter as follows:

```
convert –size 20x40 xc: none –font arggotsc.ttf  -pointsize 25
-gravity center -annotate 0,0 "L" l.gif

convert –size 20x40 xc: none –font arggotsc.ttf  -pointsize 25
-gravity center -annotate 0,0 "O" o.gif

convert –size 20x40 xc: none –font arggotsc.ttf  -pointsize 25
-gravity center -annotate 0,0 "A" a.gif

convert –size 20x40 xc: none –font arggotsc.ttf  -pointsize 25
-gravity center -annotate 0,0 "D" d.gif

convert –size 20x40 xc: none –font arggotsc.ttf  -pointsize 25
-gravity center -annotate 0,0 "I" i.gif

convert –size 20x40 xc: none –font arggotsc.ttf  -pointsize 25
-gravity center -annotate 0,0 "N" n.gif

convert –size 20x40 xc: none –font arggotsc.ttf  -pointsize 25
-gravity center -annotate 0,0 "G" g.gif
```

As you see, there is a new option called –annotate for placing letters in the middle of images. This option will take the location and letters as input.

Next, make a new canvas and use your previous image files as frames of the `.gif` animation:

```
convert -delay 0 -size 150x70 xc:white -delay 60 -page +5+15 l.gif
-page +35+15    o.gif -page +55+15 a.gif -page +75+15 d.gif -page
+95+15 i.gif -page +105+15 n.gif -page +135+15 g.gif -loop 0
loading.gif
```

The first line of this command creates an empty white area in which the animation frames will be placed. The next line sets the interval between the frames. The bunch of lines that start with the -page option will display an image containing a letter at the position specified in the parameters. Here is the syntax:

```
-page widthxheight{+-}x{+-}y
```

Width and height define the image dimensions and x and y are used for addressing the image location on the current canvas.

Finally –loop 0 means we want to repeat this animation infinitely. This animation gives the appearance of the word **loading being typed one letter at a time**.

As it is not possible to show animation on paper, I'll try to display some frames of this animation. In Fig 6-2, alternate frames of the entire animation are displayed.

Fig 6-2: Selected Frames of the Typing Effect Animation

# Workshop II: Animated Logo

Here we will study the -dispose previous option. For this workshop we need a logo and a circular text as shown in the following figure:

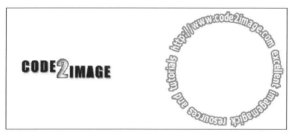

Fig 6-3: The Required Images for this Workshop

 For circular typing you can use applications like Adobe Photoshop CS or Macromedia Freehand. We need the empty area of the circular comment to be transparent. Hence, after doing suitable settings we have to save the result in the .png or .gif format

The goal of this workshop is to rotate the circular comment around the logo.

Enter the following command and make a .gif file:

```
convert -page 200x200 -size 200x200 xc:white -delay 0 -page
200x200+0+0 logo.jpg -dispose previous -delay 100 -gravity center  -
draw 'rotate 45 image over 200,200 0,0 comment.png' -gravity center
-draw 'rotate 90 image over 200,200 0,0 comment.png' -gravity center
-draw 'rotate 135 image over 200,200 0,0 comment.png' -gravity
center  -draw 'rotate 180 image over 200,200 0,0 comment.png' -gravity
center  -draw 'rotate 225 image over 200,200 0,0 comment.png' -gravity
center  -draw 'rotate 270 image over 200,200 0,0 comment.png' -gravity
center  -draw 'rotate 315 image over 200,200 0,0 comment.png' -gravity
center  -draw 'rotate 360 image over 200,200 0,0 comment.png' -loop 0
animated_logo.gif
```

The first two options of the command create a 200x200 white canvas. The third option draws the logo image immediately (`-delay 0`). But the most important option is:

```
-dispose previous
```

This option tells `convert` that every setting and drawing that we have already made should be permanent as the background of the following frames.

Would you like to see what code we have to write if we want to implement this situation without the `-dispose previous` option? Here it is:

```
convert -delay 0 -dispose none -page 200x200 -size 200x200 xc:white
-delay 0 -page 200x200+0+0 logo.jpg -delay 100 -gravity center  -draw
'rotate 45 image over 200,200 0,0 comment.png' -delay 0 -dispose none
-page 200x200 -size 200x200 xc:white -delay 0 -page 200x200+0+0 logo.
jpg -delay 100 -gravity center  -draw 'rotate 90 image over 200,200
0,0 comment.png' -delay 0 -dispose none -page 200x200 -size 200x200
xc:white -delay 0 -page 200x200+0+0 logo.jpg -delay 100 -gravity
center -draw 'rotate 135 image over 200,200 0,0 comment.png' -delay
0 -dispose none -page 200x200 -size 200x200 xc:white -delay 0 -page
200x200+0+0 logo.jpg -delay 100 -gravity center -draw 'rotate180 image
over 200,200 0,0 comment.png' -delay 0 -dispose none -page 200x200 -
size 200x200 xc:white -delay 0 -page 200x200+0+0 logo.jpg -delay 100
-gravity center -draw 'rotate 225 image over 200,200 0,0 comment.png'
-delay 0 -dispose none -page 200x200 -size 200x200 xc:white -delay 0
-page 200x200+0+0 logo.jpg -delay 100 -gravity center -draw 'rotate
270 image over 200,200 0,0 comment.png' -delay 0 -dispose none -page
200x200 -size 200x200 xc:white -delay 0 -page 200x200+0+0 logo.jpg -
delay 100 -gravity center -draw 'rotate 315 image over 200,200 0,0
comment.png' -delay 0 -dispose none -page 200x200 -size 200x200 xc:
white -delay 0 -page 200x200+0+0 logo.jpg -delay 100 -gravity center -
draw 'rotate 360 image over 200,200 0,0 comment.png' -loop 0 animated_
logo.gif
```

The second code example not only has more commands, but also produces a jerky animation with poor quality. Which code do you prefer?

Analyzing the options used in the first command, the option `-delay 100` sets the interval between frames and after that drawing of the circular comment begins. Finally the last option of that command ensures that the animation is repeated forever and saves it in a `.gif` file format as `animated_logo.gif`.

Fig 6-4: The Final Animation Mixing Two Pieces of Text

 By decreasing the rotate degree during drawing rotated text and increasing the number of commands for drawing that text we obtain an animated GIF with more frames and smoother rotation.

Till now we have studied the `none` and the `previous` parameters of the `-dispose` option in practical examples. In the next workshop we will see the use of the `background` parameter.

# Workshop III: Animated Artistic Effects

In this workshop we will apply some artistic effect on selected areas of a background image and apply transition effects to it.

Insert some vertical text in your desired image at the lower right corner and make a rectangle background around it:

```
convert  thelook.tif -fill darkblue -pointsize 20 -stroke "#f6f3ed"
-strokewidth 2 -gravity southeast -draw "rotate -90 text 0,0 'Take a
closer look at our workshops'" -channel RGBA -blur 0x3 -box "#451234"
-gravity southeast -draw "rotate -90 text 0,0 'Take a closer look at
our workshops'" thelook.jpg
```

All colors selected for the text and background drawings of this image are optional. You can choose your own colors based on your image. In this command we first set the size of text, its stroke color, and thickness and then write the stroked text and make it blur using `-channel RGBA -blur 0x3`. Finally we overwrite the sharp and clear blue text on it. The result is saved as the `look.jpg` file.

Fig 6-5: Writing Vertical Text on the Image

Now write the following code to create a seven frames GIF animation file:

```
convert -delay 0 -size 480x440 -page 480x440 xc:none -draw "image
over 0,0,0,0, 'back.jpg'" -dispose background -delay 5 -page
480x440+0+0 'back.jpg -region 130x65+135+70 -paint 8 -border 1 -
region 60x440+420+0 -spread 14 -page 480x440+0+0 'back.jpg -region
130x65+135+70 -paint 6 -border 1 -region 60x440+420+0 -spread 10  -
page 480x440+0+0 'back.jpg -region 130x65+135+70 -paint 4 -border 1
-region 60x440+420+0 -spread 7 -page 480x440+0+0 'back.jpg -region
130x65+135+70 -paint 4 -border 1 -region 60x440+420+0 -spread 4 -
page 480x440+0+0 'back.jpg -region 130x65+135+70 -paint 1 -border 1
-region 60x440+420+0 -spread 2 -page 480x440+0+0 'back.jpg -region
130x65+135+70 -border 1 -loop 0 transition.gif
```

In this command the -dispose background option is used so before every frame is drawn, the background will be replaced with the whole frame.

Then at the rectangular area from (135,70) to (265,135)—the eyes region—a paint effect will be assigned and at the rectangular area from (420,0) to (480, 440)—the text region—a spread effect will be run.

This process is repeated six times and in the last repetition just the rectangle around the eyes will be drawn so the eyes and the text come from unclear mode to a sharp state. This animation will repeat again because the -loop option is set to zero.

Fig 6-6: Some Frames of our Animated GIF

This animation plays fast and immediately restarts from the beginning. It is better to have a small pause at the last frame.

For implementing this situation we just need to insert a delay before the last frame. So we can rewrite the previous code as follows:

```
convert -delay 0 -size 480x440 -page 480x440 xc:none -draw "image over
0,0,0,0, '9.jpg'" -dispose background -delay 5 -page 480x440+0+0 9.jpg
-region 130x65+135+70 -paint 8 -border 1 -region 60x440+420+0 -spread 14
-page 480x440+0+0 9.jpg -region 130x65+135+70 -paint 6 -border 1 -region
60x440+420+0 -spread 10 -page 480x440+0+0 9.jpg -region 130x65+135+70 -
paint 4 -border 1 -region 60x440+420+0 -spread 7 -page 480x440+0+0 9.jpg
-region 130x65+135+70 -paint 4 -border 1 -region 60x440+420+0 -spread
4 -page 480x440+0+0 9.jpg -region 130x65+135+70 -paint 1 -border 1 -
region 60x440+420+0 -spread 2 -delay 300 -page 480x440+0+0 9.jpg -region
130x65+135+70 -border 1 -loop 0 transition.gif
```

There is one final hint that will be useful in this workshop. As you see there are many regions in the frames of the previous animation in which pixels are unchanged. Being able to identify pixel changes between frames and optimize animation playback by displaying just these changes is very helpful. The -deconstruct option will do this for us. Using this option at the end of all animation frames will save changed areas in each frame and saves a lot of resources during playback:

```
convert -delay 0 -size 480x440 -page 480x440 xc:none -draw "image over
0,0,0,0, '9.jpg'" -dispose background -delay 5 -page 480x440+0+0 9.jpg
-region 130x65+135+70 -paint 8 -border 1 -region 60x440+420+0 -spread
14 -page 480x440+0+0 9.jpg -region 130x65+135+70 -paint 6 -border
1 -region 60x440+420+0 -spread 10 -page 480x440+0+0 9.jpg -region
130x65+135+70 -paint 4 -border 1 -region 60x440+420+0 -spread 7 -page
480x440+0+0 9.jpg -region 130x65+135+70 -paint 4 -border 1 -region
60x440+420+0 -spread 4 -page 480x440+0+0 9.jpg -region 130x65+135+70
-paint 1 -border 1 -region 60x440+420+0 -spread 2 -delay 300 -page
480x440+0+0 9.jpg -region 130x65+135+70 -border 1 -loop 0 -deconstruct
transition.gif
```

# How to make Complex Animations

Suppose we want to make an animation that contains multiple animated clips. For example, an animation with a burning fire in the center, a moving text teaser on the bottom, a rotating logo on the top left corner, and so on.

For implementing such animations we need the frames of each clip extracted and saved as a standalone file. There are several ways for splitting an animated file into frames. In this section we will study them together.

# How to Split an Animation into Frames

The simplest way to do this is to use the -adjoin option. This option has no parameters and by default (as its name says) it is used to join some standalone images into a multi image file. So how can it help to split? Here is the secret. For some image formats like JPG or BMP it is impossible to save a series of images in the same file (this feature is not supported in these formats) and they will be saved as standalone files.

So we can use +adjoin to force all image formats to obey this behavior (although they are saved separated). It means that -adjoin and +adjoin act in a complementary manner. While -adjoin joins images into a multi-image file, +adjoin extracts the frames of an animated file into standalone images. The example below shows this clearly:

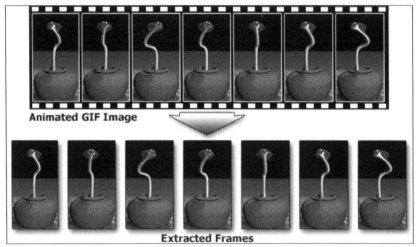

Fig 6-7: Extracting Frames of an Animated GIF using +adjoin

```
convert ani_snake.gif +adjoin snake_frame%02d.gif
```

The above command generates `.gif` files with the names `snake_frame01.gif`, `snake_frame02.gif` and so on.

> In the previous sample `snake_frame%02d.gif` is set for output names. The `%02d` means that we need a two digit sequential number to be appended at the end of the file name and the first digit is always zero. For example, `snake_frame01.gif`, `snake_frame02.gif`, `snake_frame03.gif`, and so on.

Now we have the frames extracted from the animated GIF and we are ready to use them for implementing complex scenes.

# Workshop IV: Multi-Animation Files

An important note to remember for creating such animations is that the number of all split frames of the `.gif` files should be equal to gain a smooth and good looking result. So for this workshop I choose to use eight-frame animated GIF files. The first one is the file with rotating logo (that we created in the workshop II together) and the second one is an eight-frame dancing snake animation. You may choose your own animated GIF file.

Extract the frames of these files and save them as the new images:

```
convert ani_snake.gif +adjoin snake_frame%02d.gif

convert animated_logo.gif +adjoin logo_frame%02d.gif
```

Now define a new canvas and put the corresponding frames on it:

```
convert -delay 0 -page 280x200 -size 280x200 xc: white -dispose none
-delay 0 -page 200x200+0+0 logo_frame00.gif -page 80x200+200+0 snake_
frame00.gif -page 200x200+0+0 logo_frame01.gif -page 80x200+200+0
snake_frame01.gif -page 200x200+0+0 logo_frame02.gif -page 80x200+200+0
snake_frame02.gif -page 200x200+0+0 logo_frame03.gif -page 80x200+200+0
snake_frame03.gif -page 200x200+0+0 logo_frame04.gif -page 80x200+200+0
snake_frame04.gif -page 200x200+0+0 logo_frame05.gif -page 80x200+200+0
snake_frame05.gif -page 200x200+0+0 logo_frame06.gif -page 80x200+200+0
snake_frame06.gif -page 200x200+0+0 logo_frame07.gif -page 80x200+200+0
snake_frame07.gif -loop 0 complex.gif
```

Fig 6-8: The Frames Placed beside Each Other to Make a New Animation

Now we have created a new animation with the frames of the previously created ones. What happens if we want to extract the frames of the new animated file? Let's learn that.

```
convert complex.gif +adjoin comp%02d.gif
```

And here is the output:

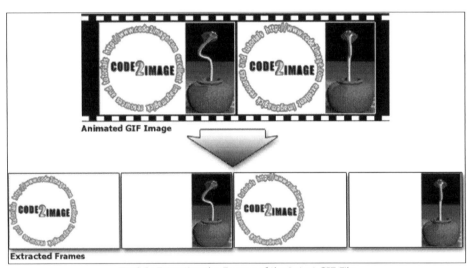

Fig 6-9: Extracting the Frames of the Latest GIF File

As you can see, the frames have been extracted differently from what we expected. On the other hand all the file names that end with an even number (for example, comp00.gif, comp02.gif, and so on) are 280x200 canvases with the logo image and all the file names that end with an odd number (for example, comp01.gif, comp03.gif, and so on) are 280x200 canvases with the snake image.

There are some problems in this scheme. First if these frames are acceptable then how we can get rid of the extra white areas? And second how can we get correct and complete frames with the logo and snake beside each other?

The command for removing extra areas is +repage. This option has no parameters and simply removes current page size and location data. So if we change the previous command as follows:

```
convert complex.gif +repage +adjoin comp%02d.gif
```

Then we get the pure frames extracted as below:

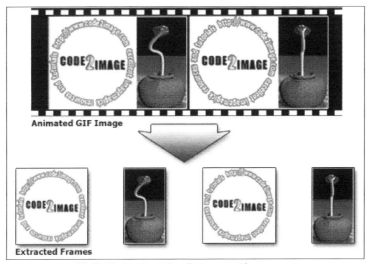

Fig 6-10: Erasing Extra Canvases with +repage

The second issue was that of split images. Suppose we want to use the constructed animation frames in another art work. Then the split images are a big problem because we have to join them manually in the new work and this will reduce play-back performance and make the animation flicker.

The coalesce option is the solution for this problem. This option merges the canvas page with the current frames and so the result is a full frame of animation and next time when we call +adjoin, the complete frames will extracted. Here is an example:

```
convert complex.gif -coalesce complex_co.gif

convert complex_co.gif +adjoin complex_frame%02d.gif
```

The output of these commands looks like this:

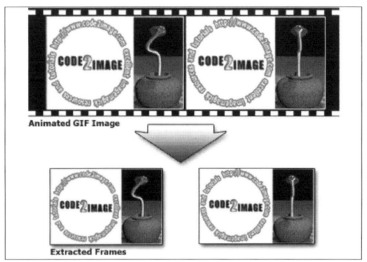

Fig 6-11: Extracting Full Frames from an Animation using -coalesce

# Summary

In this chapter we learned that there is a utility named `animate` that is used for displaying animations. This utility has a number of options that specify the display method. For creating animation, we need to use the `convert` utility. There are several techniques and manners for constructing an animated file. But there are some options that are commonly used in all of them. The most common options for making and dealing with animated files are `-delay`, `-dispose`, `-loop`, `-page`, `+repage`, `+adjoin`, `-coalesce`, and `-deconstruct`, which were discussed in detail in this chapter.

In the next chapter we will study the remaining ImageMagick utilities — `conjure`, which is a command-line interpreter, and `compare`, which annotates the differences between an image and its reconstructions.

# 7
# Conjure

In the earlier chapters, we learned that besides ImageMagick command-line utilities, there are several compilers and interpreters that we can use to accomplish custom image processing tasks. ImageMagick utilities have an internal interpreter called `conjure` that is suitable for users who don't have access to any compiler or interpreter.

The `conjure` utility can process ImageMagick scripting code, which is known as MSL (Magick Scripting Language). This language is a variant of XML. As a matter of fact, every command and option is represented in the form of elements. We will study the MSL coding notations in this chapter.

The brief description of `conjure` functionality includes the following steps:

1.  First the customised image processing commands should be written in an MSL file.
2.  Then we have to call this file as a parameter using the `conjure` utility in the command line. There are some extra options in the command line for `conjure` that we will discuss.
3.  ImageMagick processes these inputs and functions based on them.

You see this process in the following diagram:

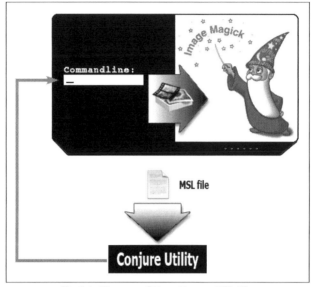

Fig 7-1: Diagram of Executing an MSL File

 As we will learn there are only few parameters for the conjure utility and the MSL elements are limited too. This means that these concepts (Conjure and MSL) are in a very early stage in the ImageMagick engine. So maybe in the next versions some changes and enhancements will be provided to them. In fact conjure is in the early stages of development as of April 2006.

As a programmer if you have any ideas for MSL and conjure development and want to contribute your suggestions, you can post them to **magick-developers@ imagemagick.org**.

# Conjure Syntax and Options

Conjure uses the following syntax:

```
conjure [options]script.msl [[options]script.msl]
```

The script.msl file is an XML file that contains elements that instruct ImageMagick to do special tasks.

For example, in the following code we convert an image from JPEG to TIFF:

```
<?xml version="1.0" encoding="UTF-8"?>
<image>
        <read filename="test.jpg" />
        <write filename="test.tif" />
        <print output="Image format converted from JPEG to TIFF" />
</image>
```

Write this code in your favorite text editor, save it as test.msl, and see it in action when you invoke it using the conjure utility as follows:

```
conjure test.msl
```

If you notice the conjure usage notation, there are some options in the command. In fact, these options perform the same task as the options in the batch files.

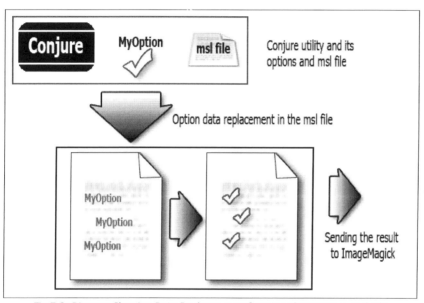

Fig 7-2: Diagram Showing Data Replacement of conjure Options in a .msl File

In a batch file execution we can define some external parameters and values that will be used by the batch file during run time. The options in the MSL files do the same. The keywords in the MSL file are replaced by the options from the command line.

Here is an example. Write the following code in a text editor and save it with the name `swirl.msl`:

```
<?xml version="1.0" encoding="UTF-8"?>
<image>
<read filename="%[inputfile]" />
<swirl degrees="%[myeffect]" />
<print output= "The file %[inputfile] swirled about
%[myeffect] degrees.\n
And the result saved as twisted.png" />
<write filename="twisted.png" />
</image>
```

Now use it on your desired image as follows:

```
conjure -inputfile myimage.jpg -myeffect 220 swirl.msl
```

That command will twist the input image by 220 degrees and save it as `twisted.png` and will print a two line output message at the command line:

```
The file myimage.jpg swirled about 220 degrees.
And the result saved as twisted.png
```

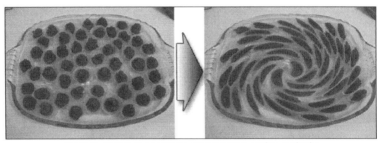

Fig 7-3: Image Processing using conjure and a .msl File

Let's take a closer look at this code. We specified two options (`-inputfile` and `-myeffect`) in the command line. For the first parameter the file name `myimage.jpg` is used and the second one has the value `220`. As I mentioned before every value of these options will be substituted for the option's name in the `.msl` file.

So the `swirl.msl` will be changed as follows before being processed by `conjure`:

```
<?xml version="1.0" encoding="UTF-8"?>
<image>
<read filename="myimage.jpg" />
<swirl degrees="220" />
```

```
<print output= "The file myimage.jpg swirled about
220 degrees.\n
And the result saved as twisted.png" />
<write filename="twisted.png" />
</image>
```

Keep in mind for naming your customized options not to use reserved keywords like debug, help, version, and verbose.

-debug:      enables and displays debug strings on output

-help:       displays conjure usage instructions on output

-version:    shows the ImageMagick version that is in use

-verbose:    prints more information about the current image

-log:        This is used with debug and specifies the content and format of output.

-monitor:    displays all errors and warning message

-quiet:      ignores to display errors and warning message

# What are the Valid Key-Value Pairs for MSL files?

Based on the current version of ImageMagick (it is 6.2.5 at the time of writing this chapter) there is a limit to the number of keys and values that we can use in MSL files.

Due to using XML notation in MSL, every element consists of a structure that starts with <element name>, content appears after that, and ends with </element name>. The table given overleaf summarizes them:

| Element | Attribute name | Description | Usage |
|---|---|---|---|
| `<image>`<br>`</image>` | `background,`<br>`color, id,`<br>`size` | Use this key for defining a new object. Every other key that will be placed between the start and end of this one will act on the current image object. We can use multiple nested `<image>` keys for implementing multi-layer or multi-paged images. In this scheme each `<image>` key matches with a `</image>`. There are 4 options for this key. The `background` and `color` options are used for setting background and foreground colors respectively; `Id` and `size` used for setting image ID and size. | `<image color="red"`<br>`background=`<br>`"#00458620">`<br>`...`<br>`</image>`<br>`<image id="3"`<br>`size="640x480">`<br>`...`<br>`</image>` |
| `<group>`<br>`</group>` | | If we need to do special tasks on a group of images, Then we can use this key. Every `<image>` key that is placed in the body of this key disposes only when we reach the `</group>` key. | `<group>`<br>`<image>`<br>`...`<br>`</image>`<br>`<image>`<br>`...`<br>`</image>`<br>`<write filename=`<br>`"image.mng" />`<br>`</group>` |

| Element | Attribute name | Description | Usage |
|---|---|---|---|
| `<read>` | `filename` | Reads a new image from a disk file. | `<read filename= "myimage.jpg" />` |
| | | | We can set to read as many images as we want to be read in the form of multiple calling this key: |
| | | | `<read filename= "file1.jpg" />` |
| | | | `<read filename= "file2.png />` |
| | | | `. . .` |
| | | | `<read filename= "filen.tif />` |
| `<write>` | `filename` | Writes the image(s) to disk. | `<write filename ="myimage.jpg" />` |
| | | | We can set to write images either as a single or multiple image files. |
| `<get>` | `height, width` | With this key we can obtain the height and width of an image and store them for later retrieval. Although this key is created for getting any attribute that the `PerlMagick` `GetAttribute()` function can recognize, for now only width and height are supported. | `<get width="img-width" height="img-height" />`<br><br>The current image height and width are stored in the `img-height` and `img-width` variables. |
| `<set>` | `background, bordercolor, clip-mask, colorspace, density, magick, mattecolor, opacity` | Sets an attribute that is listed in the previous column for the current image. All of these attributes are recognized by the `PerlMagick` `GetAttribute()` function. | |

| Element | Attribute name | Description | Usage |
|---|---|---|---|
| `<border>` | `fill, geometry, height, width` | For the current image this key draws border at the height, width, and location defined by `geometry` with thickness defined by `height` and `width` and the color that is specified in `fill`. | `<border geometery= "30x20+50+40" fill="blue" height="4" width="4"/>` |
| `<blur>` | `radius, sigma` | Blurs the current image as in the `blur` option in the Convert utility. The radius defines the range and the Sigma sets the power of blur. | `<blur radius="4" sigma="2"/>` |
| `<charcoal>` | `radius, sigma` | Adds charcoal effect to the current image as in the Charcoal option in ImageMagick. The radius defines the range and the Sigma sets the thickness of charcoal. | `<charcoal radius="6" sigma="3"/>` |
| `<chop>` | `geometry, height, width, x, y` | Removes rows and columns of pixels from the current image. The location and size of the removed area can be defined with the parameters of this key. | `<chop x="10" y="5" height="20" width="14"/>` |
| `<crop>` | `geometry, height, width, x, y` | Clips the current image at the location and size that are defined in the parameter section. | `<crop geometery== "30x20+50+40" x="15" y="15"/>` |
| `<despeckle>` | | Removes or reduces the unwanted noises and speckles from the current image. | `<despeckle/>` |
| `<emboss>` | `radius, sigma` | Acts like ImageMagick emboss option. | `<emboss radius="4" sigma="3"/>` |
| `<enhance>` | | Acts like ImageMagick enhance option. | `<enhance/>` |

| Element | Attribute name | Description | Usage |
|---|---|---|---|
| `<equalize>` | | Acts like ImageMagick `equalize` option. | |
| `<flip>` | | Acts like ImageMagick `flip` option. | `<flip/>` |
| `<flop>` | | Acts like ImageMagick `flop` option. | `<flop/>` |
| `<frame>` | `fill,` `geometry,` `height, width,` `x, y, inner,` `outer` | Acts like ImageMagick `frame` option. | `<frame fill="red"` `height="3"` `width="2"` `inner="2"` `outer="2"/>` |
| `<magnify>` | | Acts like ImageMagick `magnify` option. | `<magnify/>` |
| `<minify>` | | Acts like ImageMagick `minify` option. | `<minify/>` |
| `<normalize>` | | Acts like ImageMagick `normalize` option. | `<normalize/>` |
| `<print>` | `output` | This key prints any string that we specified in the output parameter. Using control character like \n for carriage return and line feed, is allowed. | `<print` `output="This \n is` `a \n multi line \n` `output"/>` |
| `<resize>` | `blur, filter,` `geometry,` `height, width` | Acts like ImageMagick `resize` option. | `<resize` `filter="box"` `height="30%"` `width="400"/>` |
| `<roll>` | `geometry, x, y` | Acts like ImageMagick `roll` option. | `<roll geometry=` `"40x40+100+90" x=` `"30" y="10"/>` |
| `<rotate>` | `degrees` | Acts like ImageMagick `degrees` option. | `<rotate` `degrees="45"/>` |
| `<sample>` | `geometry,` `height, width` | Acts like ImageMagick `sample` option. | `<sample` `geometry="8x5"` `height="30"` `width="10"/>` |

| Element | Attribute name | Description | Usage |
|---|---|---|---|
| `<scale>` | `geometry, height, width` | Acts like ImageMagick scale option. | `<scale geometry= "80x50" height="30" width="10"/>` |
| `<sharpen>` | `radius, sigma` | Acts like ImageMagick sharpen option. | `<sharpen radius="4" sigma="3"/>` |
| `<shave>` | `geometry, height, width` | Acts like ImageMagick shave option. | `<shave geometry="8 x1+1+1"height="8" width="10"/>` |
| `<shear>` | `x, y` | Acts like ImageMagick shear option. | `<shear x="30" y= "10"/>` |
| `<solarize>` | `threshold` | Acts like ImageMagick solarize option. | `<solarize threshold="10"/>` |
| `<spread>` | `radius` | Acts like ImageMagick spread option. | `<spread radius="4" sigma="3"/>` |
| `<stegano>` | `image` | Acts like ImageMagick stegano option. | `<stegano image= "myimage.jpg"/>` |
| `<stereo>` | `image` | Acts like ImageMagick stereo option. | `<stereo image= "myimage.jpg"/>` |
| `<swirl>` | `degrees` | Acts like ImageMagick swirl option. | `<swirl degrees= "45"/>` |
| `<texture>` | `image` | Acts like ImageMagick texture option. | `<texture image= "myimage.jpg"/>` |
| `<threshold>` | `threshold` | Acts like ImageMagick threshold option. | `<threshold threshold="10"/>` |
| `<transparent>` | `color` | Acts like ImageMagick transparent option. | |
| `<trim>` | | Acts like ImageMagick trim option. | `<trim/>` |

# Workshop I: Using Multiple MSL Files in One Conjure Call

As you see in the Conjure syntax it is possible to call the `conjure` utility with two MSL files. In this workshop we will see how to do that.

1. In your favorite text editor create an MSL file and write the following commands in it. Save this file as `sharp.msl`:

```
<?xml version="1.0" encoding="UTF-8"?>
<image>
<read filename="%[in]" />
<sharpen radius="%[rad]" sigma="%[sig]"/>
<write filename="output.tif" />
<print output= "The file %[in] sharpened\n And the result saved
as output.tif" />
</image>
```

2. Create another MSL file and write these commands in it and save it as `frame.msl`:

```
<?xml version="1.0" encoding="UTF-8"?>
<image>
<read filename="%[in]" />
<frame fill="%[framecolor]"
height="%[frameheight]"
width="%[ framewidth]"
inner="%[innerside]"
outer="%[outerside]"/>
<write filename="output.tif" />
<print output= "The file %[in] is framed\n And the result saved
 as output.tif" />
</image>
```

3. Now call these files with the `conjure` utility as follows:

```
conjure –in input.bmp –rad 4 –sig 2 sharp.msl –in output.tif
–framecolor darkgray –frameheight 3 –framewidth 3 –innerside 2
–outerside 2 frame.msl
```

Let's see what happens in these files. First of all the `sharp.msl` reads the filename in the `-in` option then sharpens the image with radius of four pixels and strength of two pixels and finally saves it as the `output.tif` file.

Fig 7-4: Sharpening an Image with sharp.msl

In the next step `frame.msl` takes the `output.tif` and makes a frame for it and saves the result as `final.jpg`. The frame color is dark gray and has a thickness of three pixels. Moreover it is two pixels thick on both the inner and outer sides.

Fig 7-5: Create a Frame for the Image with frame.msl

As you can see, all these settings are sent to `frame.msl` via external options and all value replacement takes place in the next steps.

# Compare

The last utility that we will examine is the simplest ImageMagick utility, which is used for comparing two images of the same size. When using `compare`, keep in mind that both images that are to be compared must be of the same size. Otherwise you'll get the following error message: `image size differs`.

This utility compares each pixel of the first image to the corresponding pixel of the second image and the result will be displayed numerically on screen and saved visually as an image. In the output image that contains compared pixels, all the pixel changes are marked with red. Let's see an example.

# How to Compare Two Images

The -metric option is used for mathematical and visual comparison between two images. It outputs the amount of change as its first line output and the size and format of two images as its second line. Here is an example in which a normal and sharpened image are compared:

```
compare -metric rmse normal.jpg sharp.jpg output.jpg
```

Here is the output:

```
1944.72 dB
640,320,JPEG
```

And here is the image generated after comparing:

Fig 7-6: Using the Compare Utility

# Summary

In this chapter we learned about a command-line interpreter called conjure and its scripting language called MSL (standing for Magick Scripting Language). We saw that MSL is XML and every operation in this language is done by elements.

MSL was introduced in 2002 and no serious development has been done on it yet. So if you have any idea or suggestion for MSL you can send it to the ImageMagick development team at **magick-developers@imagemagick.org**.

The last ImageMagick utility that we studied was compare. It is used for comparing two images: numerically and visually.

This chapter marks the end of the ImageMagick utilities. In the next chapter we will see some practical usage of ImageMagick, especially in web programming.

# 8

# Practical Web Projects

Some of the most important uses of ImageMagick are its web capabilities and online image processing features. We can perform almost any command-line image handling on websites too. There are two ways for calling ImageMagick from a web page:

- Installing command-line ImageMagick utilities on the server and using a **PHP** function like `exec` or `system` for running these utilities
- Installing **Magickwand for PHP** on the server and calling the library functions that Magickwand provides for image handling

Please keep in mind this is not a PHP training book and we assume you have some basic knowledge about PHP and dynamic web programming. Installing and configuring ImageMagick on a Linux server has been described before. During this chapter we assume that you've installed it on your server correctly.

## How to call ImageMagick Command-line Utilities within PHP code

There are some commands in PHP that we can use for calling external executable files (like ImageMagick command-line utilities). So by passing an ImageMagick command as a parameter to these PHP functions we can do our request online.

The popular PHP functions for executing external programs are `exec` and `system`.

 There are other functions like `passthru()`, `popen()`, `escapeshellcmd()`, and `pcntl_exec()` that can run executable files but they have lower popularity.

The `exec` function executes an external program that is specified as a parameter to it. Here is the usage format:

```
string exec ( string command [, array &output ] )
```

This function does not give any output and simply returns the last line from the result of the command. The `output` parameter is an array that will be filled with each line of output from the command. If the array already contains some elements, `exec` will append the command output to the end of the array. A sample usage of `exec` is as follows:

```php
<?php
echo exec('whoami');
?>
```

Assuming that the `whoami` command exists in the `PATH` configuration, this command outputs the username that owns the running `php/httpd` process.

The simplest form of using this function with ImageMagick is using a parameterized command utility as a parameter in it. For example:

```
exec("fullpathtoimagemagick/convert fullpathtoimage/A.jpg
fullpathtoimage/B.png)
```

Look at this command. It is very important when calling an ImageMagick utility in an `exec` command to address the correct locations of the executable and the source and destination image files. In fact most errors when using ImageMagick online come from incorrect addressing. In the previous command we have to place a valid address of where we've installed ImageMagick instead of `fullpathtoimagemagick`. Moreover the absolute address of where we are going to read and write an image should be specified in `fullpathtoimage` placeholder.

The better solution when using `exec` is to initialize some variables with the environment path of the ImageMagick command-line utilities installation and the path of where the images are going to be read and written. Here is an example:

```
exec("$CONVERT $filename ".$IMAGES.$id."_1.jpg");
```

In this command, `$CONVERT` is a UNIX path to the `convert` utility (for example, `/usr/bin/convert`). The variable `$IMAGES` contains the path to where the output file is to be stored, and the variable `$filename` contains a temporary file or the full UNIX path to the original file. The PHP `system` command can also be used for executing external programs. It has a similar syntax to `exec`. However, in this chapter we will use `exec` for our workshops.

The examples provided in this chapter don't need a large amount of memory and the default memory size specified in the `php.ini` file is enough. You can change the memory size by editing the `php.ini` file if it is required.

# How to Save the Result of an Online Image Processing Task

Let's look at the required steps for online image processing using ImageMagick. First we need a form that takes user inputs, including text and image. By clicking on a submit button these inputs should be sent to another page where ImageMagick utilities and commands are waiting to do their task.

After making an artwork successfully, we have to show it back to the user. This means that we need to save the image on our server space and this will be a challenge for us. If you think about the filename of the final image you'll understand what I mean.

Suppose three users send their personal settings and information at the same time for working on the same image. The question is what name we should give the resulting image.

If we overwrite the original image then we will lose it for other users and if we choose a specific name for it, then the result belongs to the last user who clicked on the submit button on our website.

The following figure represents this issue in an easier way:

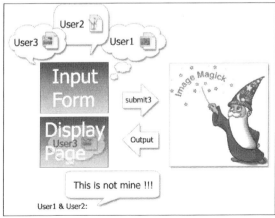

Fig 8-1: User 3 is the Last One to Press the Submit Button and hence, her/his Image Overwrites the Others

What should we do? One solution is to generate a random number for each submit action and use that number in the name of the image file generated by ImageMagick. The drawback is that the random numbers may be the same because it is possible that at the same time thousands of users press the submit button. Moreover, spending time checking for repeated numbers for each submit is not the optimum solution.

We need something unique and quick. How about using cookies in the body of file names? In this way every image file name will be generated for only one user and even if a million users work on the same image simultaneously, a million unique file names will be generated.

A cookie is specific data that a web script can generate and store on the user's computer. It can be used for tracking users and recognize them when they return to a website.

But there is an issue with using cookies. Some of the web browsers do not support cookies. Moreover sometimes users disable cookies in their browser. So our strategy for using cookies in naming image files will fail.

One of the excellent features of PHP programming is its session capabilities. There are some functions in PHP that are used to implement a session for each user who visits a web page. These functions implement cookies internally even if the browser doesn't support it or if the users disable it themselves.

# How to Start Sessions for our Visitors

There are two alternatives for activating a session for a visitor. We can simply use a PHP function called `session_start()` at the beginning of our PHP code or we can edit our `php.ini` file and add the `session.autostart` option. We will use the `session_start()` function in this chapter. The former method has its own drawbacks.

After starting a session we can access the session ID for each user through the SID constant. So it will provide us a unique file name for our artwork. We just need to add this ID number at the end of the original file name and save the result with that name. The general form of such code is something like this:

```php
<?php
Session_start();
$filename = $original_filename.strip_tags(SID);
// our required code for image processing
//we just need to use $filename variable for saving the result
?>
```

> In this piece of code the strip_tags() function strips its
> parameter of any extra data. We use it for preventing any
> cross-site attack issues.

So let's see some practical examples and study what ImageMagick and PHP can do for us.

# Building a Confirmation-Code Box

While using the Internet, especially when we are filling membership forms, sometimes they ask us to write down a jerky random alphanumeric combination into a specific field. This field has various names, but it is usually called the confirmation-code field.

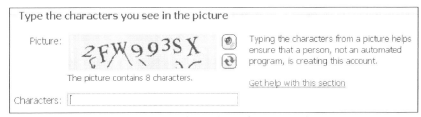

Fig 8-2: Hotmail Sample Confirmation Code

What is the reason for putting such a field in an application or membership form? On the Internet, there are too many techniques and mechanisms that professionals use for speeding up their work and increasing their benefits.

For example, a referral system requires users to fill out a long survey form and then introduce five extra buddies to be a qualified person for monthly bonuses. So if you write a program that can fill out these forms for you then you can definitely speed up this thing. To defend against these mechanisms the webmasters and web programmers provide a confirmation-code box in which due to the irregular character arrangement on a pattern or crowded background, any internet robot or form filler program cannot parse the field and hence it fails.

> Recently it was reported that the confirmation code in such
> images can be detected using advanced code. So a confirmation
> image does not prevent robots, it just makes the process difficult.

In this workshop we are going to design and develop a random confirmation-code box with the help of ImageMagick and PHP.

This workshop has two main parts. The first part is a random string generator, which produces an alphanumeric string four to fifteen characters long. This generator will be completely developed in PHP. In the second part we pass the generated string to a function that calls ImageMagick for drawing each character with a specific font, size, position, rotation, and so on.

Before writing these characters on an image file, a random patterned or colored background is generated. So let's start.

We use the `rand` function for generating random numbers and use the `chr` function for achieving a character corresponding to the given **ASCII** code. As you can see we map the generated random numbers from 48 to 57 for numbers (that is, 0 to 9), 65 to 90 for capital letters (that is, A to Z), and 97 to 122 for lower case letters (that is, a to z). The first step is to define every variable that is used in this program. This includes initializing the minimum length and maximum length, and emptying the string code:

```
$min=4;
$max=15;
$code="";
```

By using the `rand` function we will generate a random string length. We use a `for` loop for creating it:

```
for($i=0;$i<rand($min,$max);$i++)
```

Now we produce a random integer number from 48 to 122 to choose a letter corresponding to the generated **ASCII** code, but we have to be sure there are valid letters and not other characters. We can extract our required letters using a set of `if` and `else` conditions:

```
// The range of valid characters for string
$num=rand(48,122);

// The range of lower case letters
if(($num > 97 && $num < 122))
{
$code.=chr($num);
}

// The range of capital letters
else if(($num > 65 && $num < 90))
```

```
{
$code.=chr($num);
}


// The range of numbers
else if(($num >48 && $num < 57))
{
$code.=chr($num);
}


// Decrement counter
else
{
$i--;
}
}
```

In the code opposite we use the chr function for converting a number to a character. Moreover, as we want to add the generated character at the end of the previous string, we use the dot operator at the end of the string variable. For example, $code .= chr($num);

Look at the last else in that piece of code. In that block we decrement the loop counter. So if the generated ASCII code doesn't match with any valid alphanumeric character then we have to decrement the counter in order to get the right length for our string.

Save the script as randomstr.php and upload it in the same path as the web page that will call it. The complete code is here:

```
<?php
// filename "randomstr.php"
$min=4;    // minimum length of string
$max=9;    // maximum length of string
$code=""; // to store generated string


for($i=0;$i<rand($min,$max);$i++)
{


// The range of valid characters for string
$num=rand(48,122);


// The range of lower case letters
if(($num > 97 && $num < 122))
```

```
{
$code.=chr($num);
}

// The range of capital letters
else if(($num > 65 && $num < 90))
{
$code.=chr($num);
}

// The range of numbers
else if(($num >48 && $num < 57))
{
$code.=chr($num);
}

// Decrement counter
  else
{
$i--;
}
}
?>
```

The `image_creator.php` file is where the operational part of this is called. This file has two main parts. This first part uses includes to insert the code for creating random strings and creating backgrounds. The second part will work on the generated string and set size, position, and rotation specifications for each character.

```
<?php
Session_start();

// calling the random string generator here
include "randomstr.php";

// calling the random background generator here
include "bkgnd.php";

// Save the background image in a variable
$background = "background.gif";
```

```
// Save the path where convert installed in a variable
$CONVERT = "/usr/bin/convert";

// use a variable for command line contents
$CMD = "$CONVERT $background –pointsize 30 –strokewidth 1
–stroke black –fill white –gravity center";
for (i=1; i<= strlen($code); i++)
{
$Ch_size[i] = rand (15,20);
$Ch_rot[i] = rand (-10,10);
$Ch_xpos[i] = i * 30;
if( $Ch_rot > 0)
{
if ( i<= strlen($code)/2)
{
$Ch_ypos[i] = strlen(code)/(2*i);
$Ch_xpos[i] -= $Ch_xpos[i];
}
else
$Ch_ypos[i] = - (2*i)/ strlen($code);
}
else if($Ch_rot < 0)
{
if ( i<= strlen($code)/2)
{
$Ch_ypos[i] = -strlen($code)/(2*i);
$Ch_xpos[i] -= $Ch_xpos[i];
}

else
$Ch_ypos[i] = (2*i)/ strlen($code);
}
else
$Ch_ypos[i] = 0;

$CMD.= "–draw \'rotate $Ch_rot[i] text $Ch_xpos[i] $Ch_ypos[i]
\"$code[i-1]\" \' ";
}
$CMD.= " code".strip_tags(SID).".gif";
```

```
// run the command
exec($CMD);
}
```

Let's see what happens in this script. After setting a session the first four lines are used for including prewritten code and initializing variables, which will simplify the programming process.

In the next line we use a variable called $CMD for making our command body. Observing this command, we find that it can be divided into three parts:

- The first part is the section where the initial ImageMagick parameters are called. The following code is generated in the first part:

  ```
  convert background.gif –pointsize 30 –gravity center
  ```

- The middle part contains a set of similar –draw parameters. In fact in this section the –draw parameter is called several times (based on string length) with various arguments so we use a loop to simplify the code. In this code random size, vertical and horizontal position, and rotation are used for each character.

- The last part will add the name of the image that these letters are going to be written on.

We need a unique name for our image file so, by using the SID constant, we use a user session ID for naming the image file.

Finally, we run the command by calling exec and the produced image is ready to be used in a web form.

As you may notice, in the previous code a file named bkgnd.php is included at the beginning of the program. Let's take a look at this file:

```
$CMD= "/usr/bin/convert –size 250x60";
switch (rand(1,4))
{
case 1:
$CMD.="xc: blue ";
Break;

case 2:
$CMD.="gradient: yellow-blue ";
Break;

case 3:
$CMD.="plasma: fractal ";
```

```
Break;
case 4:
$CMD.="pattern: hexagons";
Break;
}
$CMD.= " background.gif"

exec($CMD);
```

This command has three parts, which deal with initializing, setting the background type based on a random number between 1 and 4 (1 = solid color, 2 = gradient, 3= plasma, 4= pattern), and saving the result in a .gif file.

After making the command body we will run it using the exec command.

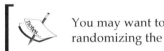

You may want to add more power to this code by randomizing the content of each case command.

The complete source of this program can be found on the download bundle on www.packtpub.com.

Here are some sample code images generated by this program.

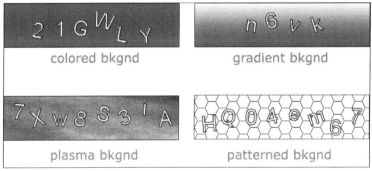

Fig 8-3: Samples from the Program Output

# Online Image Water Marking

One of the most important usages of online image processing is watermarking. A watermark is a little sign or logo that is placed on an image to mark it as a copyrighted resource. This is a simple workshop that shows you how to place a watermark on an image with a single command call.

1. Design your logo or sign that you are going to use as a watermark. This sign should have a transparent background for better results. The sign should be uploaded, preferably to the directory where the other images are uploaded.

Fig 8-4: The Image (Left) and the Logo (Right) that
will be Used on it as a Watermark

2. Now use the -watermark option as shown in the following code for watermarking:

```php
<?php
//initializing variables
$image= $_POST['input'];
$water= $_POST['mrk'];
$result= $_POST['output'];
// Save the path where composite installed in a variable
$COMPOSITE = "/usr/bin/composite";

if ($result == null)

// use a variable for command line contents
$CMD = "$COMPOSITE -watermark 30% -gravity southeast
 $image $water $image ";
else

// use a variable for command line contents
$CMD = "$COMPOSITE -watermark 30% -gravity southeast
 $image $water $result ";
```

```
// run the command
Exec($CMD);
?>
```

The output will look like this:

Fig 8-5: The Watermarked Image

In the code opposite we first get the input files that have been sent to our `.php` page using the POST method and save them in some variables. The path to the `composite` utility is saved in a variable (as before) to make it easier to call the ImageMagick command-line utility.

```
//initializing variables
$image= $_POST['input'];
$water= $_POST['mrk'];
$result= $_POST['output'];
$COMPOSITE = "/usr/bin/composite";
```

Next we should study the output file. We have two choices for that file. The first solution is to overwrite the watermarked image on the input file (which saves web space, but the original uploaded file will be lost):

```
if ($result == null)
// use a variable for command line contents
$CMD = "$COMPOSITE -watermark 30% -gravity southeast
$image $water $image ";
```

Another alternative is to save the watermarked image as a new file (which needs more space, but the original uploaded file will remain unchanged):

```
if else
// use a variable for command line contents
$CMD = "$COMPOSITE -watermark 30% -gravity southeast
$image $water $result ";
```

To use this code save it as a PHP file (`wmark.php` for example) and simply send the image name, watermark, and if you wish output file as its parameters as shown below:

```
http://www.yourdomain.com/samples/wmark.php?input=statue.jpg&mrk=c2i.
gif &output=copyrighted_statue.jpg
```

or:

```
http://www.yourdomain.com/samples/wmark.php?input=statue.jpg&mrk=c2i.
gif
```

# Summary

In this chapter we saw how to use ImageMagick with PHP to add some useful functions to your website. We saw how to make life harder for spammers with a confirmation-code generator, and how to stamp your site's mark on all the images you serve with a watermark feature.

In the next two chapters, we'll continue looking at ImageMagick and PHP. We're going to create an application for generating e-cards and other fun combinations of text and graphics.

# 9

# An E-Card Application

E-cards and websites that provide customized digital images like posters, flash clips, and animated or still e-cards have attracted internet users' attention during recent years. There are several technologies used for implementing this group of art works.

You can implement them using **Macromedia Flash** (or using other flash-like applications, for example, **koolmove, swishmax**, and so on) or you can build them using the internal PHP graphic library known as **GD**.

In this chapter we will see how to use ImageMagick for creating them. But before starting please keep the following notes in mind:

- ImageMagick or other graphic libraries and applications are just tools with some capabilities for creating various graphics like poster, e-cards, and so on. Familiarity with these packages is required but not enough. The more important factor is having good knowledge and creativity when it comes to selecting image, text, font, color, and any other artistic concept that may help in creating excellent and amazing artwork.

- Due to the subject of this book (ImageMagick) and our need for e-card elements like fonts and images we have to refer to some image and font websites. Moreover, we need to install downloaded fonts and define them for ImageMagick. I've introduced links to various websites offering free collections of fonts, animated GIFs, and images in Appendix A. The required steps for installing new fonts for ImageMagick are described in Appendix A. I would recomend you to go through Appendix A before proceeding further with this chapter.

- This workshop unlike previous ones consists of a few sections. In each part a unique creative technique for implementing a professional e-card is discussed.

- And finally we have three similar steps for creating customized e-cards. First we need a web form in which the user will select the image source. The image may come from a current web image gallery, an off-site URL, or it can be uploaded from the user's computer to the website. At the second step the user inputs (including texts and other settings) are received and sent to the image processing page by clicking the **Submit** button. At the next step a session is implemented in a PHP page and after doing any necessary image processing the user's session ID is used for creating a unique file name and finally the created artwork will be displayed to him or her. This process will be implemented as a three-step wizard.

# Wizard Step 1: How to Receive Images

The first step involves deciding on an image source. There are three possible resources for input images:

- Current web image gallery
- Off-site image URLs
- Images uploaded by user

So the first step will need the following code in order to create a selectable resource page:

```
<html>
<head>
<title>My Ecards</title>
<meta http-equiv="Content-Type" content="text/html; charset=windows-1256">
<META content="MSHTML 6.00.2900.2802" name=GENERATOR>
</head>
<body bgcolor="#ffffff" leftmargin="0" topmargin="0" marginwidth="0" marginheight="0">
<font face="Times New Roman, Times, serif" size="6" color="#777777">
<strong>Customized E-Cards Wizard.</strong> </font><br>
<font size="3" face="Arial, Helvetica, sans-serif" color="#545454">
<strong>  STEP 1. S E L E C T   T H E   S O U R C E</strong>
</font>
<hr>
<br>
```

```
<table align="center" width="600" cellpadding="0" cellspacing="0">
<tr align="center">
<td>
<a href="gallery.htm" target="mainframe">
Web Image Gallery</a>
</td>
<td>
<a href="url.htm" target="mainframe">
Off-site Image URL</a>
</td>
<td>
<A accessKey=n href="upload.htm"  target="mainframe">
Upload Your Image</A>
</td>
</tr>
<tr>
<td colspan="3"><hr></td>
</tr>
<tr>
<td colspan="3">
<iframe frameborder="0" marginheight="0" marginwidth="0"
scrolling="no" src="gallery.htm" height="550" width="600"
name="mainframe">
</iframe>
</td>
</tr>
</table>
</body>
</html>
```

At the first step of the wizard the image source must be specified. So an `iframe` is defined after the three possible image sources given above, which contains the images in the web gallery by default:

```
<tr>
<td colspan="3">
<iframe frameborder="0" marginheight="0" marginwidth="0"
scrolling="no" src="gallery.htm" height="550" width="600"
name="mainframe">
</iframe>
```

```
</td>
</tr>
```

Every time you choose another image source the content of the related web page will be displayed in this frame.

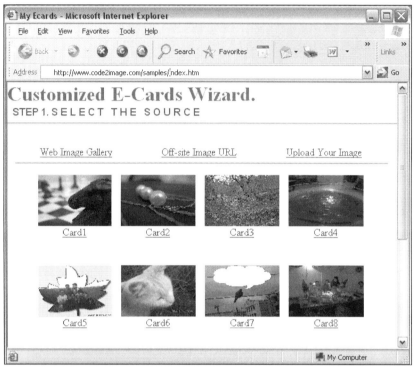

Fig 9-1: Sample Web Page that Contains some E-Card Thumbnails

The simplest method for image handling is using images that are already uploaded to the current website. Assume you have a page with several images that will be used as e-card backgrounds. We have to choose an image on which to write our personal text. This page could have the following structure:

```
<html>
<head><title>My Ecards</title></head>
<body>
<div align="center">
<table width="100%" cellspacing="5" cellpadding="5" border="0" >
<tr>
<td>
```

```
<div align="center"><a href="card1.htm">
<img src="images/card1.jpg" height="80" width="120"
border=0><br>
Card1<br></a><br>
</div>

</td>
<td>
<div align="center"><a href="card2.htm">
<img src="images/card2.jpg"  height="80" width="120"
border=0><br>
Card2<br></a><br>
</div>

</td>
<td>
<div align="center"><a href="card3.htm">
<img src="images/card3.jpg"  height="80" width="120"
border=0><br>
Card3<br></a><br>
</div>

</td>
<td>
<div align="center"><a href="card4.htm">
<img src="images/card4.jpg"  height="80" width="120"
border=0><br>
Card4<br></a><br></div>

</td>
</tr>
<tr>
<td>
<div align="center"><a href="card5.htm">
<img src="images/card5.jpg"  height="80" width="120"
border=0><br>
Card5<br></a><br>
</div>

</td>
```

```
<td>
<div align="center"><a href="card6.htm">
<img src="images/card6.jpg"  height="80" width="120"
border=0><br>
Card6<br></a><br>
</div>

</td>
<td>
<div align="center"><a href="card7.htm">
<img src="images/card7.jpg"  height="80" width="120"
border=0><br>
Card7<br></a><br>
</div>

</td>
<td>
<div align="center"><a href="card8.htm">
<img src="images/card8.jpg"  height="80" width="120"
border=0><br>
Card8<br></a><br>
</div>

</td>
</tr>
</table>
</div>
</body>
</html>
```

 You can edit this code and add any necessary elements to it based on your personal requirements.

Clicking on an image should lead us to a page containing a form for getting the required input texts from the user. We have several pages. In fact there is a unique page for each image. The reason that we cannot use the same page for these images is that each image has its own characteristics. So it is up to you as a designer to choose font, size, color, and other design factors for each image. Moreover, based on the empty space on the image and other settings, you need to have various webpages for image processing.

For example if you choose card7 the page has the following contents:

```
<html>
<head><title>My Ecards</title></head>
<body>
<FORM action=step3.php method=post>
<TABLE cellSpacing=0 cellPadding=2 border=1 >
<TR>
<TD colspan=2 align=center>
<INPUT type=hidden name="final_image" value="card7.jpg">
<img src=card8.jpg border=0>
</TD>
</TR>
<TR>
<TD >
<INPUT name="msg_1stline" maxLength=25 size="30">
</TD>
<TD >
First line of the message:<br>
  (you have to write it with maximum 25 characters)
</TD>
</TR>
<TR>
<TD>
<INPUT name="msg_2ndline" maxLength=25 size="30">
</TD>
<TD >
Second line of the message: <br>
(you have to write it with maximum 25 characters)
</TD>
</TR>
<TR>
<TD>
<INPUT type=submit value="submit">
<INPUT type=reset value="clear">
</TD>
```

```
</TR>
</TABLE>
</FORM>
</body>
</html>
```

 Keep in mind that we can implement this page in any static or dynamic form. This is just simple html code to show you the overall process of making an e-card.

This code will generate a page like the one shown below. Due to balloon size on the image we can write a two line message for the image.

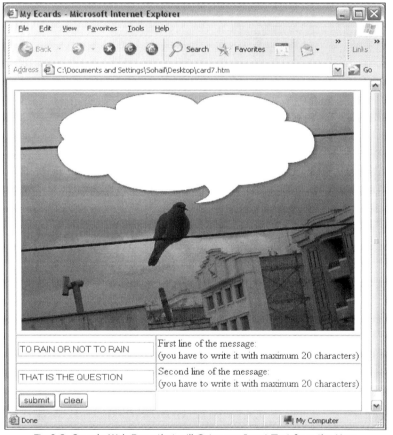

Fig 9-2: Sample Web Form that will Get some Input Text from the User

By clicking on the **Submit** button, the image and the required two line text will be sent to the `step3.php` page. As a designer you have to set up a suitable setting for font, size, and color (for each prepared image). So in `step3.php`, predefined charactristics will be applied to the image and the result will be generated and displayed as below:

Fig 9-3: Output of step3.php for image7.jpg

The `step3.php` page is the place that contains various predefined/userdefined settings for sentences in the images. Hence, the question is what mechanism does it need to distinguish a web gallery image from a URL or uploaded one?

Before answering this question, let us see what happens if we choose another source for the input image.

# How to Receive Images from URLs

Another option in the first step of the wizard is referring to an image which is located on an off-site URL. So we need a form that specifies a URL address. This form may contain the following tags:

```
<html>
<head><title>My Ecards</title></head>
<body>
<div align="center">
```

```
<table width="100%" cellspacing="0" cellpadding="0" border="0" >
<tr>
<td >
<div align="left">
Enter your image url here:
</div>

</td>
</tr>
<tr>
<td>
<form method="post" name="myform" action="step2.php")>
<input type="text" size="75" name="url" >
<input type="submit" value=" » " >
</form>
</td>
</tr>
</table>
</div>
</body>
</html>
```

Write this code in a simple text editor, save it as `url.htm`, and upload it in the same path where the first page of the wizard is located. Then if you click on the **Off-site Image URL** link, the content of `url.htm` will be displayed in the first page frame:

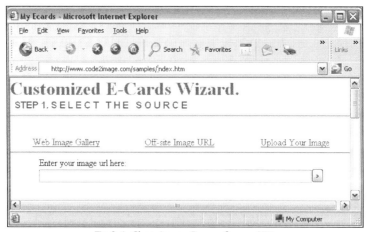

Fig 9-4: Choosing an Image from a URL

After entering the image URL and pressing the button after it (that is the button which is labeled with the » character), that image will be sent to `step2.php`.

> When addressing an image from an off-site URL, be careful! Sometimes because of security issues webmasters prefer to block their website contents (including images) from being accessed from outside. This feature is called **Hotlink Protection** and can be activated via the website's control panel. When this feature is activated images are not shown via URL addressing.

# How to Upload Images

The third method for working on images is uploading them from your computer to the server. So we need another page that contains a form for uploading the image to the server.

Clicking on the **Upload Your Image** link will display a form that contains the following commands:

```
<html>
<head><title>My Ecards</title></head>
<body>
<div align="center">
<table width="100%" cellspacing="0" cellpadding="0" border="0" >
<tr>
<td >
<div align="left">
Select the image file from your computer
</div>

</td>
</tr>
<tr>
<td align="center">
<form action="upload.php" method="post"
enctype="multipart/form-data">
<input type="file" name="myfile"><br>
<input type="Submit" value="upload">
</form>
</td>
```

```
</tr>
</table>
</div>
</body>
</html>
```

This piece of code will generate a web page in which we have a **Browse** button (i.e. `<input type="file" name="myfile">`) to locate our image.

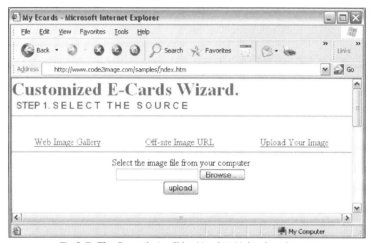

Fig 9-5: The Page that will be Used to Upload an Image

 You may notice that the sample pages generated based on code I provided in this chapter are simple. In fact they have CSS-free black text on a white background and the links in them use the default color definition. For your personal use you can define your favorite styles in a CSS file and include it in your code.

Pressing the **upload** button sends the image name to a PHP page that uploads it to the server. Here is the content of the `upload.php` file:

```php
<?php
// we assume that your image will be uploaded at the current path of
// upload.php file and in the subfolder which is specified in
// $image_upload_dir variable.
// you can define any folder name you wish. Moreover multi-depth
// subfolders are allowed too.
$image_upload_dir = "uploaded_images/";
```

```php
// check if the directory exists or not. If folder doesn't exist an
// error message will be displayed.
if (!is_dir("$image_upload_dir"))
{
die ("The directory <b>($image_upload_dir)</b> doesn't exist");
}
// The function is_writeable() returns true if the directory is
// writable. Otherwise an error message will be displayed
if (!is_writeable("$image_upload_dir"))
{
die ("The directory <b>($image_upload_dir)</b> is NOT
writable. Refer to that directory and define access
mode 777 for it");
}
// With the is_uploaded_file('filename') we can check to see if
// a file has been selected and uploaded with a temporary name
if (!is_uploaded_file($_FILES['myfile']['tmp_name']))
{
echo "Error!!!";
exit();
}
// The variable $filename contains the value of the file name
// submitted from the form.
$filename =  $_FILES['myfile']['name'];
// Before saving the temporary image data to the target, we have to
// check if file already exists with the file_exists() function
if(file_exists($image_upload_dir.$filename))
{
echo "Warning!!! The file <b>$filename </b>already exists";
exit();
}
// The function move_uploaded_file('filename','destination') Moves
// image data as a new file to a new location.
if (move_uploaded_file($_FILES['myfile']['tmp_name'],
$image_upload_dir.$filename))
{
// If this function returns true we should inform
// the user
```

```
echo "File (<a href=
step2.php?resource=./$image_upload_dir$filename>$filename
</a>) uploaded!</br>";
// File name is a link to step2.php page which uses file name
// and its path as input resource
echo "click on the file name to write your text on it.</br>"
exit();
}
else
{
//Print error
echo "There was a problem copying your file";
exit();
}
?>
```

We have implemented the information receive phase and are ready to customize the image that we have chosen.

# Wizard Step 2: How to Write Text on Input Images

We saw that the images in the web gallery have various predefined settings for writing text on them, but what about other images?

So we need a page to define new charactristics for fonts that we are going to use on the image text. `step2.php` contains several parts for defining these settings and a unique naming mechanism for files. As we saw in the earlier discussions in this chapter we can create unique file names using user session IDs.

The first problem is to obtain the overall properties of the image that is addressed or uploaded. We have no idea about the format and size of the image that the user is going to work on and hence it is necessary to get information like:

- What is the image dimension?
- How long is the text (after font specifications are defined) that the user is going to write?
- How big is the area the user is going to write the text on?

When the user knows the image dimensions, then he or she has better estimation about what portion of the image is suitable for work and how big an area he or she can use for writing the text.

We need some code to check these issues otherwise the final image may have the wrong text alignment.

A PHP file called `identify_image.php` can help us obtain the height and width of the images:

```php
<?php
if(empty($settings)){
// define an array for image charactristics
array $im_specs[];

// store image path and name
$working_image = POST_['resource']

// Save the path where identify is installed in a variable
$identify = "/usr/bin/identify";

// obtain image width and height
$CMD = "$identify –format \"%w\n%h\" $working_image";
exec($CMD, $im_specs[]);
}
?>
```

The variable `$settings` is used here to figure out if the code is running for the first time. I am going to use `identify_image.php` in the body of `step2.php` so I'll provide a better description of the `$settings` variable in the next paragraphs.

Let's take a closer look at the line that runs the ImageMagick command. As you know from Chapter 5, the `format` parameter in `identify` can be used to extract specific charactristics from an image. Here the `%w` and `%h` are used to obtain image width and height respectively. Between these control characters a `\n` is used to print them on separate lines. Why? Because the `exec()` command has an array parameter that contains every single line of the command output as its element.

Do you remember the `exec()` command usage?

```
string exec ( string command [, array &output ] )
```

The output parameter is an array that will be filled with every line of output from the command. If the array already contains some elements, exec() will append the command output to the end of the array.

So after executing the following lines:

```
// obtain image width and height
$CMD = "$identify -format \"%w\n%h\" $working_image";
exec($CMD, im_spec[]);
```

The im_specs[0] element will contain width and im_specs[1] will contain the height of the image. Let's see how we can use them to convey the image size to the user.

 In the same manner it is possible to extract other image specifications from an image.

# How to Show Image, Image Size, and the Required Fields for Writing Text

The first step for implementing step2.php is activating a session for the user and then including the previous PHP file (identify_image.php). We have to show the image and other fields for creating some text on it and the final part of step2.php has some code to generate an image with some text on it. So this file may contain the following general form:

```
<?php
Session_start();
// Computing width and height of image
include 'identify_image.php';
// initializing variable with form fields
$txt1=POST_['line1'];
$txt2=POST_['line2'];
$txt3=POST_['line3'];
$txt4=POST_['line4'];
$txt5=POST_['line5'];
$fname=POST_['font_name'];
$fsize=POST_['font_size'];
$fcolor=POST_['font_color'];
$X=POST_['x_pos'];
$Y=POST_['y_pos'];
```

```
?>
// creating the page
<html>
<head>
<title>My Ecards</title>
<meta http-equiv=Content-Type content=text/html;charset=windows-1256>
<META content=MSHTML 6.00.2900.2802 name=GENERATOR>
</head>
<body bgcolor=#ffffff >
<font face=Times size=6 color=#777777>
<strong>Customized E-Cards Wizard.</strong> </font><br>
<font size=3 face=Arial color=#545454>
<strong>  STEP 2. W R I T E   S O M E
  T E X T</strong>
</font>
<hr><br>
<?php
// Displaying the form for the first time
if(empty($settings)){
$settings = 1;
$output_image = strip_tags(SID).$working_image;
?>
<table width=800 cellpadding=0 cellspacing=0>
<tr align=center>
<td align=left>
<form method=post name=data action=$PHP_SELF>
1st line:<input name=line1 size=25><br>
2nd line:<input name=line2 size=25><br>
3rd line:<input name=line3 size=25><br>
4th line:<input name=line4 size=25><br>
5th line:<input name=line5 size=25><br>
Font name:<input name=font_name size=15><br>
<font face=Tahoma size=1 color=#777777>Select a
name between Arial, Tahoma, Times</font><br>
Font Size:<input name=font_size size=15><br>
<font face=Tahoma size=1 color=#777777>Enter a
```

```
number between 1-99 for text size</font><br>
Font color:<input name=font_color size=15><br>
<font face=Tahoma size=1 color=#777777>Select a
color name like: Black, Blue,...<br>

or enter a hex number like: #a789f1</font><br>
Text X position:<input name=x_pos size=4><br>
Text Y position:<input name=y_pos size=4><br>
<br>
<input type=submit value=submit>
</form>

</td>
<td align=center valign=middle>
<font face=Tahoma size=2 color=#666666>
.$im_spec[0]."<br>
$im_spec[1].<img src=".$working_image." border=0
align=absmiddle>
</font>
</td>
</tr>
</table>
<?php
// Save the path where convert is installed in a variable
$convert = "/usr/bin/convert";
// Create the output image
$CMD= "$convert ".$working_image." -fill ".$fcolor. "-pointsize
".$fsize." -draw \"text ".$X.",".$Y." ".$txt1."\n" .$txt2."\n"
.$txt3."\n" .$txt4."\n" .$txt5.\" .$output_image;
exec($CMD);
}
// displaying the form testing other settings
// or confirm the image
else{
?>
<table width=800 cellpadding=0 cellspacing=0>
<tr align=center>
<td align=left>
<form method=post name=data >
```

```
1st line:<input name=line1 size=25><br>
2nd line:<input name=line2 size=25><br>
3rd line:<input name=line3 size=25><br>
4th line:<input name=line4 size=25><br>
5th line:<input name=line5 size=25><br>
Font name:<input name=font_name size=15><br>
<font face=Tahoma size=1 color=#777777>Select a
name between Arial, Tahoma, Times</font><br>
Font Size:<input name=font_size size=15><br>
<font face=Tahoma size=1 color=#777777>Enter a
number between 1-99 for text size</font><br>
Font color:<input name=font_color size=15><br>
<font face=Tahoma size=1 color=#777777>Select a
color name like: Black, Blue,...<br>
or enter a hex number like: #a789f1</font><br>
Text X position:<input name=x_pos size=4><br>
Text Y position:<input name=y_pos size=4><br>
<br>
<input type=hidden name=final_image value=
".$outputimage."
<input type=submit value=again?
onClick=(data.action=$PHP_SELF)>
<input type=submit value=confirm
onClick=(data.action=step3.php)>
>
</form>
</td>
<td align=center valign=middle>
<font face=Tahoma size=2 color=#666666>
.$im_spec[0]."<br>
$im_spec[1].<img src=".$output_image."
border=0 align= absmiddle>
</font>
</td>
</tr>
</table>
<?php
// Save the path where convert is installed in a variable
```

```
$convert = "/usr/bin/convert";
// Create the output image
$CMD= "$convert ".$working_image." -fill ".$fcolor. "-pointsize
".$fsize." -draw \"text ".$X.",".$Y." ".$txt1."\n" .$txt2."\n"
.$txt3."\n" .$txt4."\n" .$txt5.\" .$output_image;
exec($CMD);
}
echo "</body>";
echo "</html>";
?>
```

There is a conditional block in this code that may need some more description. Here is the `if` clause. The content of this section of code is run if it is the first time we are referring to the code. This is figured out by checking the contents of the `$settings` variable. This variable is set to 1 to inform that we have visited this page already:

```
// Displaying the form for the first time
if(empty($settings)){
$settings = 1;
```

Now we need to save a copy of the original image for future reference as it is possible that the user may need to test various text and settings several times on the image to get a final result. Besides if that image is an off-site one, we have no access to it and for handling such an image we need to save it with a unique name locally. So by adding a session ID at the beginning of the original image name we get a new name for it and it is ready to be saved on the server:

```
$output_image = strip_tags(SID).$working_image;
```

In the next section a form with some fields is displayed using a bunch of `echo` commands. The user can enter text and required settings in this form.

```
<table width=800 cellpadding=0 cellspacing=0>
<tr align=center>
<td align=left>
<form method=post name=data action =$PHP_SELF>
1st line:<input name=line1 size=25><br>
2nd line:<input name=line2 size=25><br>
3rd line:<input name=line3 size=25><br>
4th line:<input name=line4 size=25><br>
5th line:<input name=line5 size=25><br>
Font name:<input name=font_name size=15><br>
<font face=Tahoma size=1 color=#777777>Select a
```

```
name between Arial, Tahoma, Times</font><br>
Font Size:<input name=font_size size=15><br>
<font face=Tahoma size=1 color=#777777>Enter a
number between 1-99 for text size</font><br>
Font color:<input name=font_color size=15><br>
<font face=Tahoma size=1 color=#777777>Select a
color name like: Black, Blue,...<br>
or enter a hex number like: #a789f1</font><br>
Text X position:<input name=x_pos size=4><br>
Text Y position:<input name=y_pos size=4><br>
<br>
<input type=submit value=submit>
</form>
```

As you see the output of the form is sent to `step2.php` again (that is, the `action` parameter in the `Form` tag is set to `$PHP_SELF`). So any necessary changes can be performed if needed.

Beside this form the image that has been uploaded or addressed through an off-site URL is also displayed:

```
</td>
<td align=center valign=middle>
<font face=Tahoma size=2 color=#666666>"
.$im_spec[0]."<br>
$im_spec[1].<img src=".$working_image."
border=0 align=absmiddle>
</font>
</td>
</tr>
</table>
```

As you can see the width and height of the image are displayed as well using the `$im_spec` variables from the previous included PHP page.

If you run this code it will output a form with an image, labeling the width (at the top) and the height (at the left):

Fig 9-6: The step2.php Form when it Runs for the First Time

But we need to display another form if the step2.php page has been run before. Why? Suppose that the user has used this page and added some text to his/her desired image but then is not satisfied with the result; if we simply guided him/her to the next step (that is step3.php) she/he would have had no chance to change the image except by repeating the whole process from the beginning. The solution is provided in the else clause as follows:

```
// displaying the form to test other settings or confirm the image
else{
?>
<table width=800 cellpadding=0 cellspacing=0>
<tr align=center>
<td align=left>
<form method=post name=data >
```

```
1st line:<input name=line1 size=25><br>
2nd line:<input name=line2 size=25><br>
3rd line:<input name=line3 size=25><br>
4th line:<input name=line4 size=25><br>
5th line:<input name=line5 size=25><br>
Font name:<input name=font_name size=15><br>
<font face=Tahoma size=1 color=#777777>Select a
name between Arial, Tahoma, Times</font><br>
Font Size:<input name=font_size size=15><br>
<font face=Tahoma size=1 color=#777777>Enter a
number between 1-99 for text size</font><br>
Font color:<input name=font_color size=15><br>
<font face=Tahoma size=1 color=#777777>Select a
color name like: Black, Blue,...<br>
or enter a hex number like: #a789f1</font><br>
Text X position:<input name=x_pos size=4><br>
Text Y position:<input name=y_pos size=4><br>
<br>
<input type=hidden name=final_image value=
".$outputimage.">
<input type=submit value=again?
onClick=(data.action=$PHP_SELF)>
<input type=submit value=confirm
onClick=(data.action=$step3.php)>
</form>

</td>
<td align=center valign=middle>
<font face=Tahoma size=2 color=#666666>
.$im_spec[0]."<br>
$im_spec[1].<img src=".$output_image."
border=0 align= absmiddle>
</font>
</td>
</tr>
</table>
```

The main difference between these two forms (that is, the form in the `if` clause and the form in `else` clause) is the value of the `action` parameter in the `Form` tag. In fact there is no `action` parameter here. Instead there are three extra `<input>` tags:

```
<input type=hidden name=final_image value=
".$outputimage.">
<input type=submit value=again?
onClick=(data.action=$PHP_SELF)>
<input type=submit value=confirm
onClick=(data.action=step3.php)>
```

The first `<input>` tag is a hidden control, which contains the image produced based on last text settings. It is hidden because we don't need to see its content but in `step3.php` we do need to know the image file name to display it.

> As you may have noticed, the name of this field is the same as the hidden control in the gallery image form. So `step3.php` can act on any image coming from the website gallery, off-site URL, or an uploaded image.

The second `<input>` tag is a submit button (labled with **again?**) and if it is clicked the user will be led to `step2.php` because of this code:

```
onClick=(data.action=$PHP_SELF)
```

The third `<input>` tag is a submit button (labled with `confirm`) and if it is clicked the user will be led to `step3.php` because of this code:

```
onClick=(data.action=step3.php)
```

Pressing this button means that the current settings are approved.

Fig 9-7: Running the Page after the First
Visit causes these Buttons to Replace
the Previous one on the Form

Now the important part of the page (which is the same for both `if` and `else` sections) is the part that generates the image:

```
// Save the path where convert is installed in a variable
$convert = "/usr/bin/convert";

// Create the output image
$CMD= "$convert ".$working_image." -fill ".$fcolor. "-pointsize
".$fsize." -draw \"text ".$X.",".$Y." ".$txt1."\n" .$txt2."\n"
.$txt3."\n" .$txt4."\n" .$txt5.\" .$output_image;
exec($CMD);
```

The `$convert` variable contains the full path to the `convert.exe` utility and the `$CMD` variable is set to any text settings (including font name, size, and color and the position that the text is going to be written on the image).

Finally, the `exec` command runs the `$CMD` contents and creates the specified image.

# Wizard Step 3: Final Image

This step is pretty simple if you decide to just show the result. In fact we can implement it as a frame in the previous step. But let's do it in a new page because if someday you decide to use the final image for commercial usage (that is, sell the output as an e-card, poster, etc.) making it in a new page will help you.

The general form of `step3.php` may be as follows:

```
<?php
// initializing variable with form field
$image=POST_['final_image'];
// creating the page
?>
<html>
<head><title>My Ecards</title>
<meta http-equiv=Content-Type content=text/html; charset=windows-1256>
<META content=MSHTML 6.00.2900.2802 name=GENERATOR>
</head>
<body bgcolor=#ffffff >
<font face=Times size=6 color=#777777>
<strong>Customized E-Cards Wizard.</strong> </font><br>
<font size=3 face=Arial color=#545454>
<strong>  STEP 3. S E N D   T H E   R E
S U L T</strong>
</font>
```

```
<hr><br>
<!-- building the form -->
<table align=center  cellpadding=6 cellspacing=0>
<tr align=left>
<td>
<img src=".$image." border=0>
</td>
<TD>
<FORM name=sender action=send_image.php
method=post>
<TABLE cellSpacing=0 cellPadding=0 width=180
border=0>
<TBODY>
<TR>
<TD >How would you liketo send your personal
message?<BR> <BR>
<TABLE>
<TBODY>
<TR>
<TD vAlign=top>
<INPUT type=radio CHECKED value=1
name=sender>As a Postcard</TD>
<TD >  € 3 </TD></TR>
<TR>
<TD vAlign=top>
<INPUT type=radio value=2 name=sender>
As a Poster</TD>
<TD class=text vAlign=bottom> € 7
</TD></TR>
<TR>
<TD vAlign=top>
<INPUT type=radio value=3 name=sender>
As a Download</TD>
<TD vAlign=bottom> € 1</TD></TR>
<TR>
<TD vAlign=top>
<INPUT type=radio value=4 name=sender>
As an E-Card</TD>
```

```
<TD> (free)</TD></TR>
</TBODY>
</TABLE>
</TD>
</TR>
<TR>
<TD >
<input type="submit" value="proceed"></TD>
</TR>
</TBODY>
</TABLE>
</FORM>
</TD>
</tr>
</table>
</body>
</html>
```

This code will generate a page with a form like the one shown below:

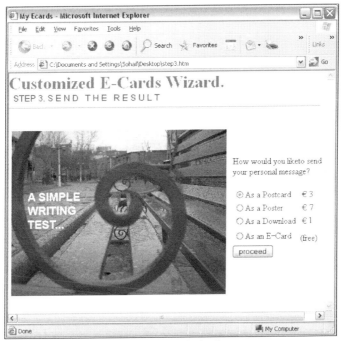

Fig 9-8: The step3.php Page

```
<FORM name=sender action=send_image.php method=post>
```

The `send_image.php` script may have several parts each of which acts based on what value is posted for the `sender` variable by the previous page form.

For the first three options you can implement a form in which user information including personal info and the payment method is gathered and saved in a predefined database.

For the money transfer process you can use financial services gates like PayPal or use direct manners like MasterCard and Visa.

The last option is a free service so you can email the generated image to your friends via the related section in the `send_image.php` page.

This means that this page must have a form for specifying sender's and receiver's names and email addresses and an optional message for the receiver. Then using the **PHP** mail function the send process must be done. It is possible to write code for storing all email addresses for future support.

As you may guess implementing `send_image.php` is your homework and I'll be very glad to answer any questions and problems you may have while developing this page. You can contact me at **info@sohail2d.com**.

# Summary

In this chapter we learned to combine text and images chosen by a visitor to your website, and produce unique designs especially for them. In the next chapter, we're going to do some exciting things with the text so that the message the reader creates ends up looking like it's a real part of the photo!

# 10

# Exciting E-Card Designs

In the previous chapter we concentrated on how to develop the required steps for implementing a wizard-based image handling process. So we had no special effects on the generated images (we just inserted some simple text in the image). In this last chapter, I'm going to show you how to use PHP code and ImageMagick functionalities for creating some amazing electronic art.

## E-card A: Simple Letters

After choosing your image write PHP code to generate graphical letters with colored background as follows. It is assumed that you've designed a complete web form with any required controls already, and that form gets the user multi-line string (in this case three lines are provided; you can expand this code to support more lines).

```php
<?php
Session_start();
//initializing variables
$message1 = POST_['msg_1stline'];
$message2 = POST_['msg_2ndline'];
$message3 = POST_['msg_3rdline'];
$backgnd = POST_['image'];
// Save the path where convert is installed in a variable
$convert = "/usr/bin/convert";
$mogrify = "/usr/bin/mogrify";
// a function for writing each line of text as a block of letters
function write_text(int $x, int $y, string $msg)
{
//create a new image with the same size as the background
//for writing the first line of the letters on
```

```php
$CMD = "$convert -size 540x400 xc:transparent line1".strip_
tags(SID).".gif";
exec($CMD);
for($i=0;$i<strlen($msg);$i++)
{
// we use mogrify because the result doesn't need to be
// written on a new image
$CMD="$mogrify line1".strip_tags(SID).".gif" -fill white -pointsize
30";
// select a random font
$FONT = rand(1,3);
Switch ($FONT){
Case 1:    $FONT=arial; break;
Case 2:    $FONT=times; break;
Case 3:    $FONT=tahoma; break;
}
$CMD.= "-box \'rgb(rand(0,200), rand(0,200), rand(0,200))\' -
font $FONT -draw \'text ".$x."+30*$i,".$y." \"$msg[$i]\"\'";
exec($CMD);
}
//create first line
Write_text(10, 40, $message1);
Write_text(10, 95, $message2);
Write_text(10, 140, $message3);
// combine the created images in a new file
$CMD = "$convert $backgnd
Line1".strip_tags(SID).".gif"
Line2".strip_tags(SID).".gif"
Line3".strip_tags(SID).".gif"
final".strip_tags(SID).".jpg";
exec($CMD);
?>
<!-- show the result to the user -->
<table width=100>
<tr>
<td align=center>
<img src= final".strip_tags(SID).".jpg border=0>
</td>
</tr>
</table>
```

Save the code as `makecard.php` in the same folder as the input form. This will enable the user's data to get placed on it by simply clicking on the submit button.

 You can call this page directly using the following URL address `http://www.yourdomain.com/makecard.php?image=back.jpg&msg_1stline=this is& msg_2ndline=just a&msg_3rdline=simple test`

I think I've to give you some explanation on this code. As before there is some initializing at the beginning and after that the main function that will write each line of text is developed. In this function there is a command that creates an image that is the same size as the background:

```
$CMD = "$convert -size 540x400 xc:transparent line1".strip_tags
(SID).".gif";
exec($CMD);
```

Then a loop repeats for the number of letters in each line. (The repetition is controlled by the `strlen` function). While running this loop, a letter with a colored background is generated and because there is no need to create new images we use the `mogrify` utility to overwrite the created letter on the previous image. As you can see each letter has a random font and background color:

```
for($i=0;$i<strlen($msg);$i++)
{
// we use mogrify because the result doesn't need to be
// written on a new image
$CMD="$mogrify line1".strip_tags(SID).".gif" -fill white -pointsize
30";
// select a random font
$FONT = rand(1,4);
Switch ($FONT){
Case 1:    $FONT=arial; break;
Case 2:    $FONT=times; break;
Case 3:    $FONT=tahoma; break;
Case 4:    $FONT=courier; break;
}
$CMD.= "-box \'rgb(rand(0,200), rand(0,200), rand(0,200))\' -
font $FONT -draw \'text ".$x."+30*$i,".$y." \"$msg[$i]\"\'";
exec($CMD);
```

Please note that the size of the background image and the location you are going to put the text on are important factors in writing the previous loops. Hence for your personal images you may need to rewrite the loops again.

After creating three images for each line of text we combine them in a new file using the `convert` utility:

```
// combine the created images in a new file
$CMD = "$convert $backgnd Line1".strip_tags(SID).".gif"  Line2".
strip_tags(SID).".gif" Line3".strip_tags(SID).".gif" final".strip_
tags(SID).".jpg";
exec($CMD);
?>
```

And finally the combined image will be shown to the user:

```
<!-- show the result to the user -->
<table width=100>
<tr>
<td align=center>
<img src= final".strip_tags(SID).".jpg border=0>
</td>
</tr>
</table>
```

Here is a sample output of this code:

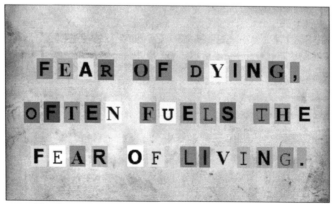

Fig 10-1: Creating Letters using the Color Box Background

# E-card B: Write on Curved Surfaces

Based on what image we are going to mix with a text there are many ways for creating the right effect. In this workshop we will experiment using a curved surface.

Firstly, you need to choose your own image with a curved element inside.

Fig 10-2: An Image with a Curved Surface Element

Now assuming you have created the required input form page and variable initialization in the next page (as shown in the previous workshop) write the following code.

```php
<?php
Session_start();
//initializing variables
$message1 = POST_['msg_1stline'];   // contains No
$message2 = POST_['msg_2ndline'];       // contains MORE
$message3 = POST_['msg_3rdline'];   // contains WAR
$backgnd = POST_['image'];
$CMD = "$CONVERT -size 130x145 -xc:black -fill:white -font beurk -
pointsize 35 -gravity north -draw \"text 0,0 .$message1.\" -draw
\"text 0,50 .$message2.\"
-draw \"text 0,100 .$message3.\" text".strip_tags(SID).".gif";
exec($CMD);
$CMD = "$COMPOSITE gradient.jpg text".strip_tags(SID).".gif" -diaplace
```

```
-8 curvedtext".strip_tags(SID)."".gif";
exec($CMD);
$CMD = "$COMPOSITE -compose copyopacity -gravity south -geometery -
10+0 urvedtext".strip_tags(SID)."".gif"Background.jpg card".strip_
tags(SID)."".jpg";
exec($CMD);
?>
<!-- show the result to the user -->
<table width=100>
<tr>
<td align=center>
<img src= ecard".strip_tags(SID)."".jpg border=0>
</td>";
</tr>
</table>
```

Fig 10-3: Creating a Simple
Text on a Black Background

As you can see we choose a font that simulates color drops fallen from a big brush. This will help make the effect better.

In the second command a previously created gradient image is used for curving the text. The negative value for -displace sets the curve downward.

Fig 10-4: Creating Curved Text with the Help of a Gradient Image

Finally, in the last command the curved text is mixed with the background at the location defined using the -gravity and -geometry options.

Fig 10-5: Placing the Text on the Rook

After compositing the text on the image it will be displayed to the user as shown in the last seven lines of our PHP code.

# E-card C: Carving Technique

Carving is the one of the amazing techniques that helps e-cards look more natural. Follow the steps provided in this workshop to implement a carving.

Choose an image that you're going to carve. I select a close-up of a red pepper and I'm going to write some text on it.

Fig 10-6: An Image with a Clear Side for Carving

Again assuming the initializing step is done, create a new file, put the text you received from the user in it, and skew it along the Y axis.

```
$CMD = "$convert -size 285x235 xc:black -fill white -pointsize 40
-font blazed -gravity north -draw\"skewY -12 text 0,0 \'Would U\nLike
2 Try\nThis little\nHottie!\'\" text".strip_tags(SID).".gif";
exec($CMD);
```

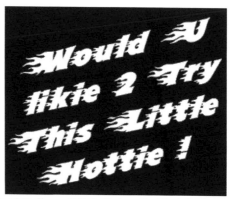

Fig 10-7: Skewed White Text on the Black Background

Now blur the text.

```
$CMD = "$convert text".strip_tags(SID).".gif -blur 0x3
blured_text".strip_tags(SID).".gif";
exec($CMD);
```

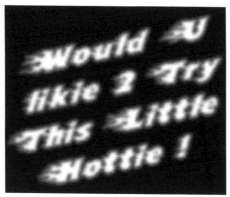

Fig 10-8: Blurred Text

Next, mix and displace the blurred text with the background image:

```
$CMD = "$composite blured_text".strip_tags(SID)."".gif background.jpg
-displace
3 displace".strip_tags(SID)."".jpg";
exec($CMD);
```

Now use a mask and extract the displaced area from the image:

```
$CMD = "$composite -compose copyopacity -gravity center
-geometry +30+45 text".strip_tags(SID)."".gif
displace".strip_tags(SID)."".jpg
carved_text".strip_tags(SID)."".gif";
exec($CMD);
```

Fig 10-9: Mask the Displaced Area

To complete the image combine the extracted and displaced text with the background:

```
$CMD = "$composite -compose multiply -gravity center
-geometery +30+45 background.jpg
carved_text".strip_tags(SID)."".gif
ecard".strip_tags(SID)."".jpg";
exec($CMD);
?>
```

Now it's time to display it back to the user:

```
<!-- show the result to the user -->
<table width=100>
<tr>
```

```
<td align=center>
<img src= ecard".strip_tags(SID).".jpg border=0>
</td>
</tr>
</table>
```

Fig 10-10: The Final Result

# How to Make Input Text more Flexible

You may have noticed that there are some limitations for text space in the previous scripts. On the other hand we have to obey the specified text size and length and number of lines specified earlier on in those workshops.

Is it possible to implement a mechanism in which the input text understands the space it has and makes any necessary changes in the size or break itself as a multi-line phrase? Yes it is possible. We just need to change the ImageMagick commands.

In the current commands we set a specific number of lines and used the -pointsize option to fix the size of input texts so that it fits into specific areas of our images.

Another alternative is using the -size and -caption options. For example, we can set the typing area as follows:

```
convert -background lightgray -size 70x120
caption:"here it is a long text" textfit.png
```

As you see a 120 pixel wide area is defined for the text and can be shown as follows:

Fig 10-11: Defined Text Area

So if the text words are extended then more lines will be used automatically:

```
convert -background lightgray -size 70x120
caption:"here it is a long text which can be resized when it needs"
textfit2.png
```

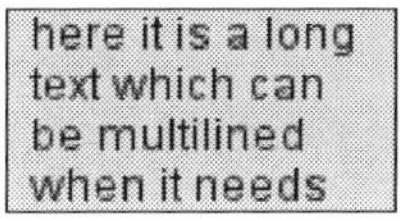

Fig 10-12: Automatic Usage of Extra Lines

# Creating a Parameterized Book Cover Generator Page

In this last workshop, I'm going to review all the tips and tricks that we have learned during this chapter. In this workshop we will design a Book Cover Generator web page in which there is a form to receive required data like:

- Book Title
- Number of Pages
- Author
- Front Image
- Back Image
- Descriptions

This cover will be produced based on the Packt Publishing cover template. So the Packt Publishing logo and its cover template will be used as the default. For your personal use you can change the code and use your preferred settings instead.

Before starting let's take a look at a sample Packt Publishing book cover:

Fig 10-13: A Sample Book Cover

So we can divide a cover into eleven parts as follows:

1. Front Cover Image
2. The **From Technologies to Solutions** slogan
3. Front Cover Book Title
4. Front Cover Brief Description
5. The Orange Band at the Cover Bottom
6. Author Name
7. Packt Publishing Logo
8. Book Title on the Spine
9. Author Name on the Spine
10. Packt Publishing Logo on the Spine
11. Comments on Back Cover

So for the first step we need a form to get this information. This form may have contents in the `cover-step1.php` script as follows:

```
<html>
<head>
<title> My Ecards </title>
<meta http-equiv=Content-Type content=text/html; charset=windows-1256>
<META content=MSHTML 6.00.2900.2802 name=GENERATOR>
</head>
<body bgcolor=#ffffff >
<font face=Times size=6 color=#777777>
<strong>Book Cover Wizard</strong> </font><br>
<font size=3 face=Arial color=#545454>
<strong STEP 1. G A T H E R I N G I N F O </strong>
</font>
<hr><br>
<!-- Displaying the form for gathering book information -->
<table width=800 cellpadding=0 cellspacing=0>
<tr align=center>
<td align=left>
<form method=post name=data action= cover-step2.php >
Image for cover:<input type=file size=38
name=cover_img><br>
Book Title:<input name=Title size=43><br>
Brief Description:<textarea name=B_Desc cols=38
rows=5 ><br><br>
Author Name:<input name=Author size=53><br>
Comments on back:<textarea name=comments cols=36
rows=5><br>
<input type=submit value=submit>
</form>
</td>
</tr>
<tr align=center>
<td align=left>
<a href=cover-template.php>change configuration</a>
</td>
</tr>
</table>
```

That code will generate a page like this:

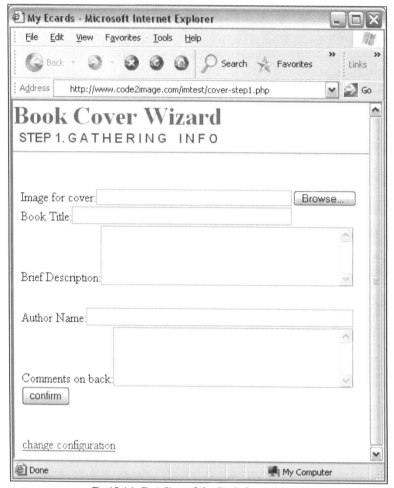

Fig 10-14: First Step of the Book Cover Wizard

 In this page the image required for the cover is uploaded by the user. You can rewrite it and choose your own manner for choosing the cover image. This image can be received by a URL and it is even possible to use current images on the server.

At the bottom of this page there is a link for predefined template configuration. We can use it to define any constant element in the cover template. For example, slogan, color box, and publication logo are parts that may never or seldom be changed. So instead of generating them for each cover we can produce them once and use them. Every time we need to add, remove, or change such elements we can go to the **change configuration** link and redefine its contents.

By clicking on this link a new page will be opened that may have the following contents:

```php
<?php
// initializing variables with form fields
$width=POST_['width'];
$height=POST_['height'];
$bk_color=POST_['bk_color'];
$slogan=POST_['slogan'];
$slogan_font =POST_['slogan_font'];
$slogan_size =POST_['slogan_size'];
$slogan_color =POST_['slogan_color'];
$slogan_bar=POST_['slogan_bar'];
$logo=POST_['logo'];
$author_bar=POST_['author_bar'];
// Displaying this page for the first time
if(empty($settings)){
$settings = 1;
}
else{
// Save the path where convert is installed in a variable
$convert = "/usr/bin/convert";
// Create the cover template
$CMD= "$convert
// template size and color
xc:".$bk_color." -size ".$widthx$height."
// slogan settings
-fill ".$slogan_bar."
-draw \"rectangle ".$width."/1.75,".$height."/1.8 ".$width.",".$heigh
t."/32\"
-pointsize ".$slogan_size."
-fill ".$slogan_color."
-draw \"text ".$width."/1.75 + 10,
".$height."/1.8 - 10 ".$slogan."\"
// logo settings
-gravity southeast
-draw \"image over ".$width." - 10,
```

```
".$height." - 10 ".$logo."\"
-gravity south
-draw \"image over ".$width." - 10,
".$height." - 10 ".$logo." Scale 90%, 90%\"
// author bar
-fill ".$author_bar."
-draw \"rectangle 0,".$height."/1.1 ".$width.",".$height."/32\"
current_template.jpg";
exec($CMD);
}
?>
<!-- creating the page -->
<html>
<head>
<title> Cover Creator </title>
<meta http-equiv=Content-Type content=text/html; charset=windows-1256>
<META content=MSHTML 6.00.2900.2802 name=GENERATOR>
</head>
<body bgcolor=#ffffff >
<font face=Times size=6 color=#777777>
<strong>Book Cover Wizard</strong> </font><br>
<font size=3 face=Arial color=#545454>
<strong T E M P L A T E S E T T I N G S</strong>
</font>
<hr><br>
<table width=800 cellpadding=0 cellspacing=0>
<tr align=center>
<td align=left>
<form method=post name=data action=$PHP_SELF>
<!-- cover dimension -->
Cover width:<input name=width size=4>
Cover height:<input name=height size=4><br>
<!-- background color -->
Background color:<input name=bk_color size=15><br>
<font face=Tahoma size=1 color=#777777>Select a
color name like: Black, Blue,...<br>
or enter a hex number like: #a789f1</font><br>
```

```
<!-- Slogan settings -->
Slogan:<input name=sloagan size=25><br>
Slogan Font:<input name=slogan_font size=15><br>
<font face=Tahoma size=1 color=#777777>Select a
name between Arial, Tahoma, Times</font><br>
Slogan size:<input name=slogan_size size=15><br>
<font face=Tahoma size=1 color=#777777>Select a
number between 1-99</font><br>
<font face=Tahoma size=1 color=#777777>For colors
Select a name like: Black, Blue,...<br>
or enter a hex number like: #a789f1</font><br>
Slogan Color:<input name=slogan_color size=25><br>
Slogan bar color:<input name=slogan_bar
size=25><br>
<!-- Publisher Logo -->
Logo image:<input name=logo size=25><br>
<!-- Author bar color -->
Author bar color:<input name=author_bar
size=25><br>
<br>
//Send new settings
<input type=submit value=Save>
</form>
</td>
<td align=center valign=middle>
<font face=Tahoma size=2 color=#666666>
current template<br></font>
<img src=current_template.jpg border=0
align =absmiddle>
</td>
</tr>
</table>
```

A preview of the current cover template settings helps us to have a clear idea of what we are going to change it to. The form located below the preview provides us with full control of the size, position, color, and contents of each element. After making any changes, click on the **Save** button to make them active.

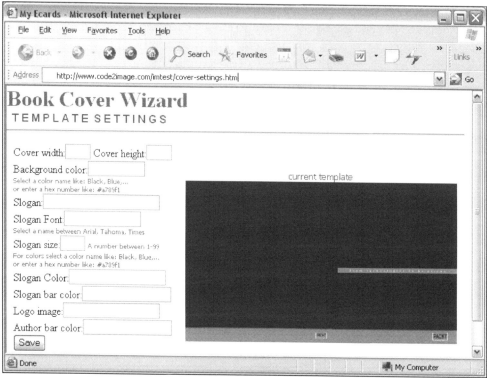

Fig 10-15: Template Configuration Page

The **Submit** button on the first page opens cover-step2.php, in which user data will be arranged and the generated cover will be displayed.

Here is the code for cover-step2.php:

```php
<?php
Session_start();
// initializing variables with form fields
$cover_img=POST_['cover_img'];
$title =POST_['Title];
$B_Desc =POST_['B_Desc'];
$Author =POST_['Author];
$comments =POST_['comments'];
array $tmpl_dim;
include('upload.php');
include('get_dim.php');
// upload the image user specified for cover
Upload_image($cover_img);
```

```php
// get template dimension
Get_dim("current_template.jpg", $tmpl_dim);
// Save the path where convert is installed in a variable
$convert = "/usr/bin/convert";
// Create the cover image
$CMD= "$convert
// the predefined template file
current_template.jpg
// draw cover image
-draw \"image over".$tmpl_dim[0]."/1.85, 0 ".$tmpl_dim[0]."- ".$tmpl_
dim[0]." /1.85," ".$tmpl_dim[1]."/1.75\"
// draw book title
-pointsize 30
-fill white
-font arial
-draw \"text ".$tmpl_dim[0]."/1.75 + 10,
".$ tmpl_dim[1]."/1.3 - 10 ".$title."\"
// draw brief description
-pointsize 10
-fill orange
-font arial
-draw \"text ".$tmpl_dim[0]."/1.75 + 10,
".$ tmpl_dim[1]."/1.35 - 10 ".$B_Desc."\"
// draw authors' names
-pointsize 15
-fill white
-font arial
-draw \"text ".$tmpl_dim[0]."/1.75 + 10,
".$ tmpl_dim[1]."/1.05 - 10 ".$author."\"
// draw back cover comments
-pointsize 10
-fill white
-font arial
-draw \"text 50,50 ".$comments."\"
my_cover".strip_tags(SID).".jpg";
exec($CMD);
}
?>
<!-- creating the page -->
```

```
<html>
<head>
<title>Cover Creator</title>
<meta http-equiv=Content-Type content=text/html; charset=windows-1256>
<META content=MSHTML 6.00.2900.2802 name=GENERATOR>
</head>
<body bgcolor=#ffffff >
<font face=Times size=6 color=#777777>
<strong>Book Cover Wizard</strong> </font><br>
<font size=3 face=Arial color=#545454>
<strong S A M P L E C O V E R</strong>
</font>
<hr><br>
<table width=800 cellpadding=0 cellspacing=0>
<tr align=center>
<td align=center valign=middle>
<font face=Tahoma size=2 color=#666666>
Sample Cover<br></font>
<img src= my_cover".strip_tags(SID)."".jpg
border=0 align =absmiddle>
</td>
</tr>
</table>
```

As usual a session is required to create a unique name at the first line of code:

```
Session_start();
```

Then some variables are initialized with data that is sent from the previous page. Moreover, we need to define an array variable because we need it to save template dimensions:

```
// initializing variables with form fields
$cover_img=POST_['cover_img'];
$title =POST_['Title];
$B_Desc =POST_['B_Desc'];
$Author =POST_['Author];
$comments =POST_['comments'];
array $tmpl_dim;
```

Next, two PHP files are included in this code. One is for uploading the image for the cover and the other for computing template dimensions:

```
include('upload.php');
include('get_dim.php');
// upload the image user specified for cover
Upload_image($cover_img);
// get template dimensions
Get_dim("current_template.jpg", $tmpl_dim);
```

 The content of these two PHP files has already been discussed earlier in this chapter.

Initializing ImageMagick's path is the next step:

```
// Save the path where convert is installed in a variable
$convert = "/usr/bin/convert";
```

The heart of this page is the line in which the convert utility with the required parameters is constructed and then run:

```
// Create the cover image
$CMD= "$convert
// the predefined template file
current_template.jpg
// draw cover image
-draw \"image over".$tmpl_dim[0]."/1.85, 0 ".$tmpl_dim[0]."- ".$tmpl_
dim[0]." /1.85," ".$tmpl_dim[1]."/1.75\"
// draw book title
-pointsize 30
-fill white
-font arial
-draw \"text ".$tmpl_dim[0]."/1.75 + 10,
".$ tmpl_dim[1]."/1.3 - 10 ".$title."\"
// draw brief description
-pointsize 10
-fill orange
-font arial
-draw \"text ".$tmpl_dim[0]."/1.75 + 10,
".$ tmpl_dim[1]."/1.35 - 10 ".$B_Desc."\"
// draw authors' names
```

```
-pointsize 15
-fill white
-font arial
-draw \"text ".$tmpl_dim[0]."/1.75 + 10,
".$ tmpl_dim[1]."/1.05 - 10 ".$author."\"
// draw back cover comments
-pointsize 10
-fill white
-font arial
-draw \"text 50,50 ".$comments."\"
my_cover".strip_tags(SID).".".jpg";
exec($CMD);
```

In the above piece of code, there are five –draw options used with a `convert` utility. As you see each -draw option places a cover element (that is text or image) in a specific location on the template file (`current_template.jpg`).

The question is how do we figure out the location of each element?

You saw that at the beginning of this code a function named `get_dim()` is used to compute template dimensions. That function outputs the width and height of a template in an array.

So by knowing the template image size, we can use a bunch of formulas to compute the location of each cover element. In this way even if a new size for original template is defined (in the **Template Settings** page), all the cover elements including text, logos, and images will be relocated automatically.

For example, if the template image is a 1000x600 file, then the location for writing the book title will be figured out as shown below.

The code formula:

```
-draw \"text ".$tmpl_dim[0]."/1.75 + 10,
".$ tmpl_dim[1]."/1.3 - 10 ".$title."\"
```

We have:

```
$tmpl_dim[0] = 1000
$tmpl_dim[1] = 600
```

So the code will be converted to:

```
-draw \"text 581,451 ".$title."\"
```

This means that the book title will be written around the (581,451) location on the template file.

 As mentioned before, these computations are based on the Packt Publishing cover template. For your own covers you have to redefine all formulas based on your needs.

Finally, the created cover will be shown to the user:

```
<!-- creating the page -->
 <html>
<head>
<title>Cover Creator</title>
<meta http-equiv=Content-Type content=text/html; charset=windows-1256>
<META content=MSHTML 6.00.2900.2802 name=GENERATOR>
</head>
<body bgcolor=#ffffff >
<font face=Times size=6 color=#777777>
<strong>Book Cover Wizard</strong> </font><br>
<font size=3 face=Arial color=#545454>
<strong S A M P L E C O V E R</strong>
</font>
<hr><br>
<table width=800 cellpadding=0 cellspacing=0>
<tr align=center>
<td align=center valign=middle>
<font face=Tahoma size=2 color=#666666>
Sample Cover<br></font>
<img src= my_cover".strip_tags(SID)."._jpg
border=0 align =absmiddle>
</td>
</tr>
</table>
```

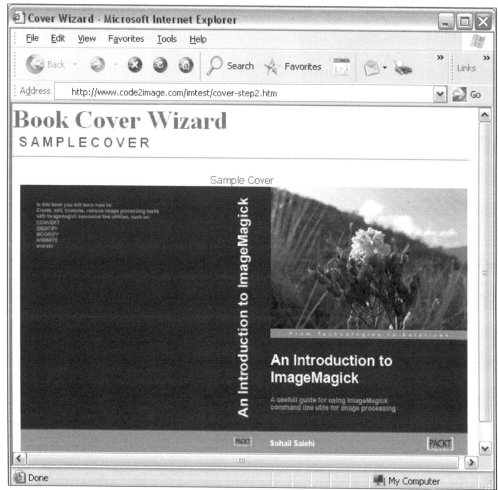

Fig 10-16: Creating and Showing the Cover Page

# Summary

In this chapter we've generated some exciting images, and seen some very powerful techniques for creating web graphics. I hope it's given you lots of ideas for your own projects. We saw how to map text onto different 3D objects, so that the text really appears to be part of the image.

We've covered a lot of ground in this ImageMagick book. I hope it was as much fun to read as it was to write. Happy Manipulations!

# A
# Install New Fonts In ImageMagick

## Why Don't Some Fonts Work Correctly?

There are many samples and workshops in this book (especially in Chapter 4) that need special fonts for writing text on images. You may notice that these samples don't work correctly on your system and although the expected image processing task is approved and the text is shown on the image, the font is not what you want and a simple default font is displayed instead.

In this appendix you will learn how to add new fonts to ImageMagick and activate them for your usage.

## How to Identify the Current Installed Fonts

Sometimes the font that you specify in your command-line code has been already installed but it is important to call it using the correct name.

If you don't know the correct name for a particular font, use the `identify` utility to see the list of installed fonts and their names:

```
identify -list type
```

Here is the sample output for Windows users:

```
Path: C:\Program Files\ImageMagick-6.2.5-Q16\type-ghostscript.xml
Name                          Family              Style    Stretch    Weight
-----------------------------------------------------------------------------
AvantGarde-Book               AvantGarde          Normal   Normal     400
AvantGarde-BookOblique        AvantGarde          Oblique  Normal     400
AvantGarde-Demi               AvantGarde          Normal   Normal     600
AvantGarde-DemiOblique        AvantGarde          Oblique  Normal     600
Bookman-Demi                  Bookman             Normal   Normal     600
Bookman-DemiItalic            Bookman             Italic   Normal     600
Bookman-Light                 Bookman             Normal   Normal     300
Bookman-LightItalic           Bookman             Italic   Normal     300
Courier                       Courier             Normal   Normal     400
Courier-Bold                  Courier             Normal   Normal     700
Courier-BoldOblique           Courier             Oblique  Normal     700
Courier-Oblique               Courier             Oblique  Normal     400
Helvetica                     Helvetica           Normal   Normal     400
Helvetica-Bold                Helvetica           Normal   Normal     700
Helvetica-BoldOblique         Helvetica           Italic   Normal     700
Helvetica-Narrow              Helvetica Narrow    Normal   Condensed  400
Helvetica-Narrow-Bold         Helvetica Narrow    Normal   Condensed  700
Helvetica-Narrow-BoldOblique  Helvetica Narrow    Oblique  Condensed  700
Helvetica-Narrow-Oblique      Helvetica Narrow    Oblique  Condensed  400
Helvetica-Oblique             Helvetica           Italic   Normal     400
NewCenturySchlbk-Bold New     CenturySchlbk       Normal   Normal     700
NewCenturySchlbk-BoldItalic   NewCenturySchlbk    Italic   Normal     700
NewCenturySchlbk-Italic       wCenturySchlbk      Italic   Normal     400
NewCenturySchlbk-Roman        NewCenturySchlbk    Normal   Normal     400
Palatino-Bold                 Palatino            Normal   Normal     700
Palatino-BoldItalic           Palatino            Italic   Normal     700
Palatino-Italic               Palatino            Italic   Normal     400
Palatino-Roman                Palatino            Normal   Normal     400
Times-Bold                    Times               Normal   Normal     700
Times-BoldItalic              Times               Italic   Normal     700
Times-Italic                  Times               Italic   Normal     400
Times-Roman                   Times               Normal   Normal     400
```

As you can see, in the first part of this command output the default fonts, which are defined during the ImageMagick installation, are listed. We will see how to change this font definition by referring to the `type-ghostscript.xml` file and editing its contents.

The second part of this command lists the fonts that have been previously installed on your platform. For example, if you are using Windows then your output will look like this:

```
Path: Windows Fonts
Name                        Family                  Style   Stretch  Weight
------------------------------------------------------------------------
02.10-fenotype             02.10 fenotype          Normal  Normal   400
02.10ital-fenotype         02.10ital fenotype      Normal  Normal   400
1942-report                1942 report             Normal  Normal   400
3D-Noise                   3D Noise                Normal  Normal   400
4YEOmonstrum               4YEOmonstrum            Normal  Normal   400
7inch-Regular              7inch                   Normal  Normal   400
7inch-Rounded              7inch Rounded           Normal  Normal   400
[.atari-kids.]             [.atari-kids.]          Normal  Normal   400
A.C.M.E.-Secret-Agent A.C.M.E. Secret Agent        Normal  Normal   400
A.M.P.                     A.M.P.                  Normal  Normal   400
Abaddon™                   Abaddon™                Normal  Normal   400
Abduction2002              Abduction2002           Normal  Normal   400
AddShade                   AddShade                Normal  Normal   400
Aharoni-Bold               Aharoni                 Normal  Normal   700
Airstream                  Airstream               Normal  Normal   400
Alfredo's-Dance            Alfredo's Dance         Normal  Normal   400
Alien-Encounters           Alien Encounters        Normal  Normal   400
Alien-Encounters-Bold Alien Encounters             Normal  Normal   700
Alien-Encounters-Bold-Italic Alien Encounters Italic  Normal   700
Alien-Encounters-Italic  Alien Encounters          Italic  Normal   400
Alpine-7558M               Alpine 7558M            Normal  Normal   400
Amped-For-Evil             Amped For Evil          Normal  Normal   400
Andalus                    Andalus                 Normal  Normal   400
Angel-Normal               Angel                   Normal  Normal   400
Anger-is-a-gift            Anger is a gift         Normal  Normal   400
Anglo-Text                 Anglo Text              Normal  Normal   400
Angsana-New                Angsana New             Normal  Normal   400
Angsana-New-Bold           Angsana New             Normal  Normal   700
Angsana-New-Italic         Angsana New             Italic  Normal   400
AngsanaUPC                 AngsanaUPC              Normal  Normal   400
```

| | | | | |
|---|---|---|---|---|
| AngsanaUPC-Bold | AngsanaUPC | Normal | Normal | 700 |
| Argor-Flahm-Scaqh | Argor Flahm Scaqh | Normal | Normal | 400 |
| YoungStar | YoungStar | Normal | Normal | 400 |
| Zebraesq | Zebraesq | Normal | Normal | 400 |
| Zebrra | Zebrra | Normal | Normal | 400 |
| Zenda | Zenda | Normal | Normal | 400 |
| ZendaEmbossed | ZendaEmbossed | Normal | Normal | 400 |
| Zippo | Zippo | Normal | Normal | 400 |
| Zoetrope--BRK- | Zoetrope -BRK- | Normal | Normal | 400 |

As you can see, in the first column is the font name that you can use in your command. The second column represents the font family that particular font belongs to. For example, **Angsana-New**, **Angsana-New-Bold**, and **Angsana-New-Italic** belong to the **Angsana New** font family.

Don't use a family name as a font name in your commands or ImageMagick will use the default font.

The third, fourth, and fifth columns are some descriptive information about font style, stretch, and size.

You need to replace every space between words of a font name with a – character. For example, the font **anglo text** should be referred as anglo-text in ImageMagick:

```
convert -size 100x100 xc:none  -font anglo-text
-pointsize 20 -draw "text 20,50 'hello'" hi.jpg
```

# Where to Find Fonts and Other Free Resources

ImageMagick is an image processing package. This means that it can handle various image elements like fonts and still images as well as animated images. Hence, **ImageMagick** users who decide to create amazing art works need to have a good archive of these elements.

The following tables briefly list some of the websites where you can find free resources like fonts, photos, and animated GIFs on the Internet.

# Free Fonts

| Website | URL |
| --- | --- |
| 1001 Free Fonts | http://www.1001freefonts.com |
| Free fonts | http://www.free-fonts.com |
| Font Freak | http://www.fontfreak.com |
| Acid Fonts | http://www.acidfonts.com |
| DaFont | http://www.dafont.com |
| CoolArchive | http://www.coolarchive.com |
| Larabie Fonts | http://www.larabiefonts.com |
| FontFile | http://www.fontfile.com |
| Simplythebest | http://www.simplythebest.net/fonts/ |
| AbstractFonts | http://www.abstractfonts.com |

# Free Photos

| Name | URL |
| --- | --- |
| Stock.xchange | http://www.sxc.hu/ |
| Flickr | http://flickr.com/ |
| Buzz net | http://www.buzznet.com/ |
| PD Photo | http://pdphoto.org/ |
| Open Photo | http://openphoto.net/ |
| Our Media | http://ourmedia.org/ |
| Free Stock Photos | http://freestockphotos.com/ |
| ImageAfter | http://imageafter.com/ |

# Free Animations

| Name | URL |
| --- | --- |
| Animation Factory | http://www.animationfactory.com |
| GIFAnimations | http://www.gifanimations.com |
| Gifs | http://www.gifs.net |
| Web Developer | http://www.webdeveloper.com/animation/ |
| Animation Library | http://www.animationlibrary.com |
| AnimatedGIF | http://www.animatedgif.net |
| Feeble Minds | http://www.feebleminds-gif.com |
| Best Animations | http://www.bestanimations.com |
| Animation Station | http://www.animation-station.com |

# How to Define New Fonts for ImageMagick

For Windows users all the True Type fonts installed on the system can be accessed by ImageMagick. As mentioned before you just need to know the right name of the font or the font family.

But Linux users need to change some settings for activating new fonts. If you specify a font in your command, ImageMagick searches it in the font configuration file, `type.xml`.

Here is the order in which the search is done:

```
$MAGICK_CONFIGURE_PATH
$MAGICK_HOME/lib/ImageMagick-6.2.4/config
$MAGICK_HOME/share/ImageMagick-6.2.4/config
$HOME/.magick/
<client path>/lib/ImageMagick-6.2.4/
<current directory>/
$MAGICK_FONT_PATH
```

Sometimes we need to add and install a new True Type font (TTF) on ImageMagick if you are a Linux user. Here are the required steps for doing this.

Copy the TTF font file to your server in the font directory (and make sure it has read and write permission).

Linux has a utility called `ttf2pt1.exe`, which converts a TTF font file to suitable font files that can be used in the system. Use this utility as follows:

```
ttf2pt1 -e ARIAL.TTF arial
```

The output of this program is two files with `.afm` and `.pfa` extensions.

The `arial.afm` file is used for metrics (size, stretch, and so on) and `arial.pfa` is the font itself that is used in Linux.

In the next step copy the `.pfa` and `.afm` files to the Ghostscript font directories. First we need to find the directory, so enter the following command to list the directories where Ghostscript looks for fonts:

```
Gs -h
```

The output of that command may look like the following:

```
/usr/share/fonts/default/ghostscript/
```

Or:

```
usr/share/fonts/default/Type1/
```

Now refer to the `Type-Ghostscript.xml` file and add a new entry to it for the new font files. For editing this file you can use the **pico** utility. As you can see, after the heading part in this file there are some `<type>` tags, using which new fonts can be defined.

Here is an example :

```
<?xml version="1.0" encoding="UTF-8"?>
<!DOCTYPE typemap [
  <!ELEMENT typemap (type+)>
  <!ELEMENT type (#PCDATA)>
  <!ELEMENT include (#PCDATA)>
  <!ATTLIST type name CDATA #REQUIRED>
  <!ATTLIST type fullname CDATA #IMPLIED>
  <!ATTLIST type family CDATA #IMPLIED>
  <!ATTLIST type foundry CDATA #IMPLIED>
  <!ATTLIST type weight CDATA #IMPLIED>
  <!ATTLIST type style CDATA #IMPLIED>
  <!ATTLIST type stretch CDATA #IMPLIED>
  <!ATTLIST type format CDATA #IMPLIED>
  <!ATTLIST type metrics CDATA #IMPLIED>
  <!ATTLIST type glyphs CDATA #REQUIRED>
  <!ATTLIST type version CDATA #IMPLIED>
  <!ATTLIST include file CDATA #REQUIRED>
]>
<typemap>
  <type
    name="AvantGarde-Book"
    fullname="AvantGarde Book"
    family="AvantGarde"
    foundry="URW"
    weight="400"
    style="normal"
    stretch="normal"
    format="type1"
    metrics="@ghostscript_font_path@a010013l.afm"
    glyphs="@ghostscript_font_path@a010013l.pfb"
    />
  <type
    name="AvantGarde-BookOblique"
```

```
      fullname="AvantGarde Book Oblique"
      family="AvantGarde"
      foundry="URW"
      weight="400"
      style="oblique"
      stretch="normal"
      format="type1"
      metrics="@ghostscript_font_path@a0100331.afm"
      glyphs="@ghostscript_font_path@a0100331.pfb"
      />
  <type
      name="AvantGarde-Demi"
      fullname="AvantGarde DemiBold"
      family="AvantGarde"
      foundry="URW"
      weight="600"
      style="normal"
      stretch="normal"
      format="type1"
      metrics="@ghostscript_font_path@a0100151.afm"
      glyphs="@ghostscript_font_path@a0100151.pfb"
      />
...
</typemap>
```

The new font should be ready to use now. Try the following command and see if it has been added to the ImageMagick default fonts:

```
identify -list type
```

# Compression In ImageMagick

## Compression versus Quality

In all the samples provided in this book we just follow a bunch of commands and set some options in them without considering factors like size, quality, and compression.

In this appendix we will take a look at the options that ImageMagick has provided for them and some hints about the best way to select an image format for our work and compress it using a suitable algorithm.

The goal of image compression is reducing the size of an image so it can be saved using less space and can be read faster especially when we are dealing with online image processing tasks.

But it definitely has its costs. By compressing an image we reduce its quality. It is up to you as a user to choose the right format and compression scheme to achieve a good balance between quality and compression. Let us see what capabilities we can find in ImageMagick for handling these issues.

## ImageMagick Options for Compression

There are two main options for working on image size and quality. The `-compress` option sets the compression algorithm that we are going to use on an image and for setting the amount of the compression and the quality of the generated image we can use the `-quality` option.

This is not as simple as mentioned here. In fact, there are some limitations on the usage of these two options. Some formats cannot accept some types of compression so we cannot use all of the `-compress` option parameters for all image formats. Moreover, the `-quality` option works only on lossy compression algorithms.

Before describing the parameters of these two options and for better understanding of these options let's study the compression types.

# Lossy versus Lossless Compression Algorithms

The image compression algorithms can be divided into two main groups. An algorithm in which the original image data will remain unchanged after compression and decompression phases is called a lossless algorithm. **LZW** and **RLE** are the most famous types of lossless algorithms. These algorithms are mainly used on image formats that contain a color palette like .gif, .png and so on

The main limitation in these formats is the number of colors. The colors in each channel cannot exceed 256. So these formats are not suitable for saving true-color images. Also for saving images with non-uniform adjacent pixels these formats are not optimal.

In contrast for saving images with solid background or minimum number of colors they considerably optimize the image size and displaying speed.

In the following figure you can compare several versions of two images, which are saved in the .gif, .png, and .jpg formats.

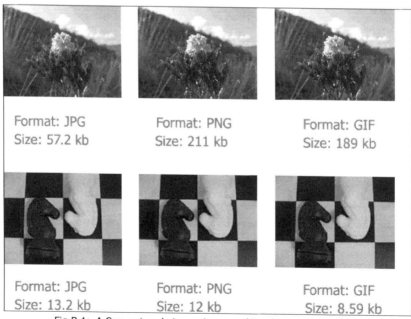

Fig B-1: A Comparison between Lossy and Lossless Image Formats

In a lossy compression algorithm, due to the quality that we have specified for compression, some of the image data will be omitted. This will produce more compression and the resulting image will have a smaller size than with the lossless methods. You may imagine that eliminating some image data will reduce the quality and generate a poor noisy image. In fact although we lose some data from the original image, due to the internal algorithm of lossy compressions the changed or lost pixel color will not be noticeable.

In the following image you can see and compare two levels of quality for creating .jpg images from a raw .bmp file. As you can see the changed pixels can be recognized if we focus on them.

Fig B-2: A Comparison between Lossy Image Formats and Raw Data

# ImageMagick –compress and –quality Options

Now let us see what capabilities ImageMagick offers for lossy and lossless compression. Here is the -compress option:

```
-compress type
```

We can use one of the following parameters for type—None, BZip, Fax, Group4, JPEG, JPEG2000, Lossless, LZW, RLE, or Zip.

The None parameter corresponds to the +compress option and will store the binary image in an uncompressed format.

Other options correspond to the format that supports them. For example, when you are dealing with a .gif file set the -compress option with the LZW parameter. Or when you are dealing with the .tif or .jpg format the JPEG scheme is suitable.

Don't worry about the right parameter for your image formats. If you don't use -compress option in your commands, ImageMagick simply chooses the appropriate compression scheme for it. That's why we skipped the –compress option in our previous workshops.

The –quality option has the following format and is used mainly for the JPEG family compression type:

```
-quality value
```

For the value we can place numbers between 0 (poor quality) and 10 (high quality). If you don't use the –quality option in your commands then the quality of the input image is used for processing or the value of 7.5 is used.

Beside formats like .jpg and .mpg this option can set the quality for the .miff and .png image formats too.

For .png files with a transparency channel, we have to define two quality values. Besides image data quality, the quality for the alpha channel is needed and can be specified as follows:

```
-quality xxxyyy
```

In this command xxx and yyy are numbers between 0 and 100. The xxx will refer to the quality of the alpha channel and yyy will be used for quality of the image data itself.

# Index

# M

Magick Scripting Language. *See* **MSL**
**Make command 24**
**Makefiles**
  about 22
  creating, GNU configure used 22, 23
**mask image**
  about 65
  creating 66
**matte channel**
  about 64
  -channel option 65
  +matte option 65
  -matte option 65
  -separate option 65
**mogrify utility, ImageMagick**
  border command-syntax 58
  label command 59
  Mogrify command 60
  options 55
  syntax, 55
  the card, workshop 56, 57, 58, 59
**montage, ImageMagick feature 8**
**montage utility, ImageMagick**
  about 61, 75
  -background option 82
  -bordercolor option 81
  -compose option 83
  creating indexed image web page, work-
     shop 87, 88
  -frame option 81
  -geometry option 84
  -matte option 81
  -mode option 86, 87
  Montage adornment options, workshop
  81, 83
  Montage arrangement options, workshop
  84-86
  Montage descriptive options, workshop
  77, 78, 80
  -null option 86
  options 75
  popular options 77
  -shadow option 81

  syntax, 75
  -texture option 82
  -tile option 85
  -title option 80
  valid parameters 75, 77
**MSL**
  about 119
  key-value pairs for MSL files 123
  MSL files, key-value pairs 128
  multiple MSL files used, Conjure calling 129
**multifunctioning, ImageMagick feature 8**

# O

**online image processing using ImageMagick**
  cookies used 136
  steps 135
**online image water marking, workshop**
  about 143
  code explanation 145
  placing water mark on an image 144, 145
  -watermark option 144, 145

# P

**painting methods, ImageMagick**
  about 33
  bordercolor parameter 35
  color filling with -draw option, workshop
  33, 35, 36
  -draw option 34
  font parameter 34
  fuzz parameter 35
  point parameter 34
  reset parameter 36
  stroke parameter 34
**PHP functions**
  exec 134
  running executable files 133
  session_start 136
  system 133

# R

**rows and columns, inserting and deleting**
  -chop option 48
  -splice option 47, 48

# Thank you for buying
# ImageMagick Tricks

## Packt Open Source Project Royalties

When we sell a book written on an Open Source project, we pay a royalty directly to that project. Therefore by purchasing ImageMagick Tricks, Packt will have given some of the money received to the ImageMagick project.

In the long term, we see ourselves and you—customers and readers of our books—as part of the Open Source ecosystem, providing sustainable revenue for the projects we publish on. Our aim at Packt is to establish publishing royalties as an essential part of the service and support a business model that sustains Open Source.

If you're working with an Open Source project that you would like us to publish on, and subsequently pay royalties to, please get in touch with us.

## Writing for Packt

We welcome all inquiries from people who are interested in authoring. Book proposals should be sent to authors@packtpub.com. If your book idea is still at an early stage and you would like to discuss it first before writing a formal book proposal, contact us; one of our commissioning editors will get in touch with you.

We're not just looking for published authors; if you have strong technical skills but no writing experience, our experienced editors can help you develop a writing career, or simply get some additional reward for your expertise.

## About Packt Publishing

Packt, pronounced 'packed', published its first book "Mastering phpMyAdmin for Effective MySQL Management" in April 2004 and subsequently continued to specialize in publishing highly focused books on specific technologies and solutions.

Our books and publications share the experiences of your fellow IT professionals in adapting and customizing today's systems, applications, and frameworks. Our solution-based books give you the knowledge and power to customize the software and technologies you're using to get the job done. Packt books are more specific and less general than the IT books you have seen in the past. Our unique business model allows us to bring you more focused information, giving you more of what you need to know, and less of what you don't.

Packt is a modern, yet unique publishing company, which focuses on producing quality, cutting-edge books for communities of developers, administrators, and newbies alike. For more information, please visit our website: www.PacktPub.com.

**PUBLISHING**

## Building Websites with Joomla!

ISBN: 1904811949    Paperback: 340 pages

A step-by-step tutorial to getting your Joomla! CMS website up fast

1. Walk through each step in a friendly and accessible way

2. Customize and extend your Joomla! site

3. Get your Joomla! website up fast

## Mastering Mambo

ISBN: 1904811515    Paperback: 304 pages

A professional-level guide to Mambo's mostpowerful and useful features

1. Build e-commerce stores and discussion forums into Mambo

2. Make your site multilingual, accessible, and optimized for speed and search engines

3. Master DOCMAN, the document manager for Mambo, to turn your Mambo site into a dynamic repository of shared documents and files

4. Create custom layouts, modules, Mambots, and more

Please check **www.PacktPub.com** for information on our titles

15600670R00123

Made in the USA
Lexington, KY
06 June 2012